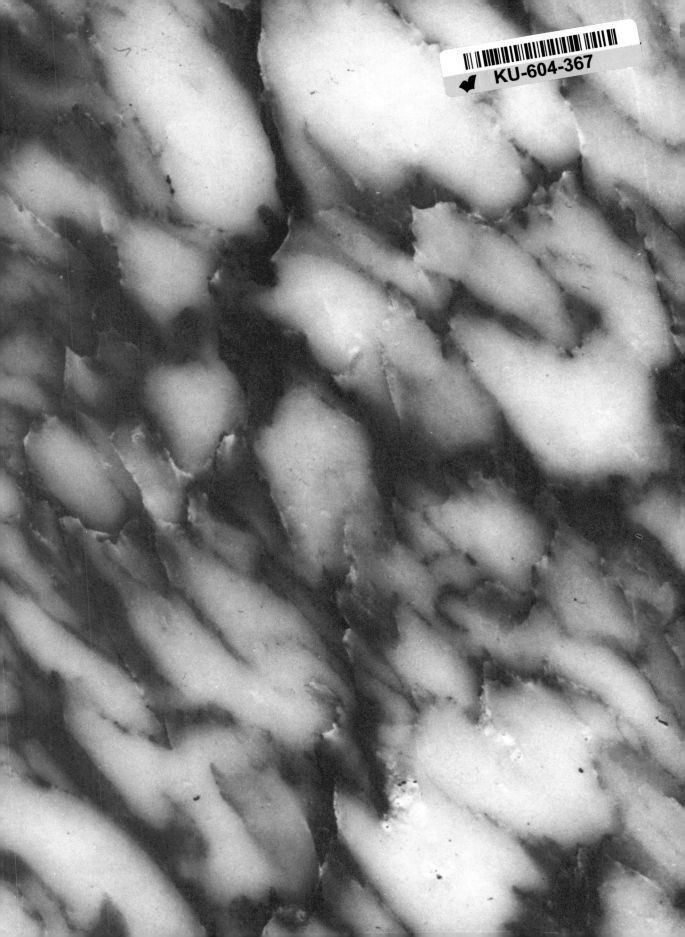

New Junior Encyclopedia

News Publishers Ltd.

Contributors

Neil Ardley B.Sc.
A. L. Barrett
N. S. Barrett M.A.
Carole Berkson
Lucy Berman B.A.
A. S. Butterfield
Ronald L. Carter B.Sc.(Econ), F.R.G.S.
Ann Clark
John O. E. Clark B.Sc., A.R.I.C.
J. N. Cleaver M.A.
T. G. Cook M.A.
Jean Cooke
Tom Edwards
Jill R. Girling B.A.
Peter Grey
R. J. W. Hammond
Brendan Hennessy
L. James M.A., Ph.D.
Robin Kerrod
Ann Kramer
Jo Logan
K. E. Lowther M.A.
Keith Lye B.A., F.R.G.S.
L. H. Munby M.A.
Dominic Recaldin B.Sc., Ph.D.

Theodore Rowland-Entwistle F.R.G.S.
G. E. Satterthwaite F.R.A.S.
D. S. Sehbai M.A.
D. Sharp L.R.A.M.
G. M. Weston B.A.
B. G. Wilson
Michael E. Wright B.A.

© 1974 Macdonald & Co (Publishers) Ltd, London.
Distributed in U.K. by arrangement with
City Magazines, 1-3 Wine Office Court, Fleet Street, London.
Distributed in Australia and New Zealand by
Bay Books (Pty) Ltd, Sydney.
Made and printed in Great Britain by
Purnell & Sons Ltd, Paulton.

Local governments organize rubbish collection from houses. Today people are becoming more and more worried about the amount of refuse produced.

Radio Many people contributed to the development of radio—there is no one single inventor. The existence of radio waves was predicted by the British mathematician Clerk Maxwell in the middle of the 19th century. Hertz, a German scientist, was the first man to generate radio waves—that was in 1888. The first 'wireless' message is claimed to have been sent across a laboratory by the Russian scientist Popov in 1896. Later that year the first experiments aimed at turning radio into a practical communication medium were carried out by Marconi in the garden of his father's villa in Italy. Several years later, Marconi astounded the scientific world by transmitting a message across the Atlantic from Cornwall to Newfoundland—a feat thought to be impossible.

Radio waves are generated by oscillatory electric currents. An important characteristic of them is their frequency which is the number of oscillations a second. Each station has its own particular frequency. A tuned circuit in the receiver selects the particular station we want. This circuit consists of a coil of wire and a component known as a *capacitor* which resonates at, and therefore gives preference to, one particular frequency. Varying the value of the capacitor alters the resonant frequency and therefore the station to which the receiver is tuned. The radio signal selected by the tuned circuit is very weak and must be amplified up to many times its original strength before it can operate a loudspeaker. Amplification is provided by transistors or radio valves (tubes). A receiver also has a valve (tube) or transistor that extracts the voice or music from the radio wave.

The heart of a radio transmitter is a

Model circuit diagram showing the components of the transistor radio receiver, including capacitors (C), resistors (R), transistors (T) and transformers (TR). An incoming signal starts at the aerial and finishes up as an audible sound at the loudspeaker at the other end.

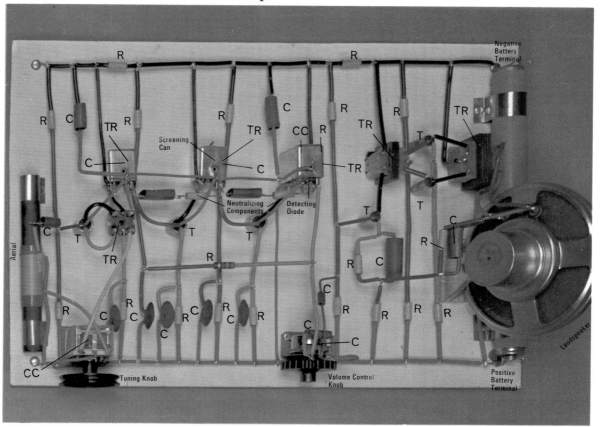

valve (tube) or transistor that generates an oscillatory current of precisely controlled frequency. The vibrations of a piece of quartz are normally used to control the frequency. After being amplified several times, the current is fed to the antenna which converts it into a radio wave.

Before reaching the antenna, however, the speech, music or telegraph signals to be carried by the radio wave are impressed on it by a process known as *modulation*. In one technique, the amplitude of the radio wave is made to vary in step with the variations in the amplitude of the speech or music. This is known as *amplitude modulation* (AM). In an alternative technique, which gives better quality, the frequency of the radio waves varies in step with the variations of the speech or music. Although this variation is not big enough to affect the tuning of the radio to the station. This is called *frequency modulation* (FM). Telegraph signals can either switch the radio wave on and off or switch its frequency back and forth between two valves.

Strange though it may seem, radio waves travel only in straight lines. Transatlantic transmissions are possible because the radio waves are bounced round the curvature of the Earth by the ionosphere (see Atmosphere). This is a layer of electrically charged (ionized) gases in the upper atmosphere. They are ionized by radiation from the Sun. Only short waves which cannot carry TV are reflected in this way. Today, telecommunications satellites in orbit round the Earth are used to relay microwave signals carrying TV programmes around the world.

Microwaves are also used on the ground to carry the many thousands of telephone conversations and TV programmes between large cities.

Radioactivity was first discovered by Henri Becquerel in Paris in 1896. He had noticed that some undeveloped photographic plates had been fogged by being left in contact with a bottle of uranium ore. Becquerel concluded after some experiments that the uranium was giving off radiations. Today we know that the atoms of radioactive elements such as uranium and radium are continually disintegrating, and can give off three kinds of radiation. In two of these *alpha particles* (written α particles) and *beta particles* (written β particles) are given off. An alpha particle consists of a group of two protons and two neutrons, while a beta particle is identical to an electron. Both types of particle come from the atom's nucleus. (See Atom.) A third kind of radiation, called *gamma rays*, does not consist of particles. Gamma rays are like very penetrating X-rays.

There can be several kinds of the same atom, called *isotopes*, and many of these are also radioactive. Atoms of carbon, for example, have a number of isotopes which differ only in the number of neutrons contained in their nuclei (plural of nucleus). Some radioactive isotopes give off only alpha particles. Others give off beta particles. Still others give off both. Today radioactive isotopes can be made artificially for use in industry and medicine. Such isotopes are made by exposing carbon, iodine and other elements found in nature to strong radioactivity in special 'ovens' or *reactors* using uranium.

Scientists working in plants where radioactive isotopes are being made and used must be protected by special clothing. They also carry small badges or *dosimeters* containing strips of photographic film. At the end of a day's work

Talking points
* Describe the difference between AM (amplitude modulation) and FM (frequency modulation). Why does FM give better reproduction than AM?
* How is it that short wave radio transmissions can be made direct across the world while medium and long wave transmissions need to have communications satellites to relay the signals?

* It could be said that the invention of radio has made the world much smaller. Discuss the enormous differences that radio has made to the world and how it has brought people closer together.
Articles to read
Communications; Crystals; Electricity; Quartz; Marconi; Satellites; Television; Transistors.

the film is developed to see if a dangerous 'dose' of radiation has fogged it.

Radioactivity can be detected by *geiger counters*. A small tube contains two metal electrodes connected with an amplifier and a voltmeter, and sometimes a loudspeaker. Radioactive particles passing through the tube cause an electric current to flow, which gives a reading on the voltmeter. The presence of radiation can also be heard as a series of clicks from the loudspeaker.

In medical research scientists can tell what is happening in the brain and other organs of the body using radioactive isotopes. Radioactive iodine, for example, can be injected in very small quantities into the bloodstream. From there the isotope is absorbed by the thyroid glands. By placing a geiger counter near the throat, the isotope can be detected as it is being absorbed by the thyroid. In this way more can be learned about the thyroid, which influences our rate of growth.

One of the many interesting uses of radioactive isotopes in industry is in the detecting of blocks in oil pipelines. A small plug called a 'go-devil' is put into one end of the pipeline. The flow of oil carries the go-devil to the block, where it stops. In the go-devil a tube of radioactive isotope has been placed. All that has to be done is to move along the length of the pipeline with a geiger counter, which will start clicking at the exact spot where the go-devil has come to a stop.

As atoms of a radioactive element disintegrate they change or *decay* to atoms of another element. Atoms of uranium decay eventually to atoms of lead. The time that it takes for half of the atoms to change or *decay* to atoms of another element is called the *half-life period*. This ranges from a fraction of a second for some radioactive elements to many many millions of years for others. The artificial radioactive isotope sodium-24 has a half-life period of 15 hours. During this time half of the atoms in one gram of sodium-24

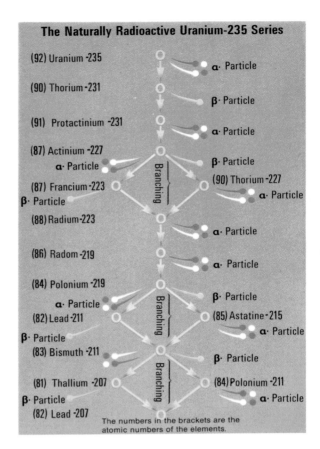

The Naturally Radioactive Uranium-235 Series

The numbers in the brackets are the atomic numbers of the elements.

Above: Atoms of the naturally-occurring isotope uranium-235 decay radioactively into atoms of another element by emitting charged particles from their nuclei. But instead of decaying into stable atoms, they decay into atoms which are themselves radioactive. These atoms in turn decay into different atoms and the process continues until a stable atom is reached — in this case atoms of lead-207. A system where atoms decay through a series of elements in this way is called a *radioactive series*. There are three entirely separate radioactive series found in nature — the uranium-238, the uranium-235 and the thorium-232 series.

Below: The half-life period of a radioactive isotope is the time taken for half of the atoms in a sample to decay to atoms of another element. For sodium-24 this is 15 hours. For uranium-238 the half-life period is nearly 5,000,000,000 years.

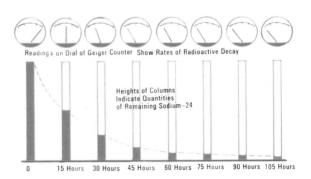

Readings on Dial of Geiger Counter Show Rates of Radioactive Decay

Heights of Columns Indicate Quantities of Remaining Sodium-24

0   15 Hours   30 Hours   45 Hours   60 Hours   75 Hours   90 Hours   105 Hours

would decay to atoms of magnesium, leaving half a gram of the radio-active isotope. During the next 15 hours half of the remaining atoms of sodium-24 would decay, leaving one-quarter of a gram of the radioactive isotope, and so on.

Archaeologists are sometimes able to use the half-life period to measure the age of historic objects made of once-living materials, such as wood. Carbon-14 is a naturally occurring radioactive isotope of carbon found in living things. By measuring the carbon-14 content in an old wooden object and comparing it with the content in a piece of new wood, the age of the wooden object can be calculated. *Radio-carbon dating*, as this process is called, was used in studying the Dead Sea Scrolls.

Radio astronomy is a branch of astronomy in which radio waves sent out by stars or clouds of matter are studied.

Radio waves are sent out by all galaxies and many stars, including the Sun. These waves are invisible, and so cannot be discovered by ordinary telescopes. But they can be picked up by receiving aerials, just like any radio broadcast. The waves start small electric currents flowing in the aerial. These currents can be turned into sound. But it is more usual, when picking up radio waves from space, to use specially designed receivers, in which the currents are automatically recorded

Some strong sources of radio signals and the time they take to reach the Earth:
1. Sun (8 minutes)
2. Jupiter (40 minutes)
3. Hydrogen gas in spiral arms of our galaxy (1,500-80,000 years)
4. The Crab Nebula—a supernova (5,000 years)
5. Supernova in Cassiopeia (10,000 years)
6. Centre of our galaxy (30,000 years)
7. Magellanic clouds (200,000 years)
8. Galaxy in Andromeda (2 million years)
9. Elliptical galaxy in Virgo (33 million years)
10. A radio galaxy in Cygnus (546 million years)

on a paper strip as a wavy line. These receivers are called *radio telescopes*. They are extremely large in order to capture as many radio waves from space as possible.

Some big radio telescopes have a large bowl-shaped reflector or 'mirror' which can be moved to point at any area of the sky. The reflector may be hundreds of feet across, like the one at Jodrell Bank, in Cheshire. In front of the reflector is an aerial on which all the waves are drawn together so that the currents they produce are large enough to be recorded.

A radio telescope 1,000 feet across has been built in Puerto Rico, in the West Indies, by lining the walls of a volcanic crater with polished aluminium.

Radio telescopes can detect far more distant objects than ordinary telescopes. Radio astronomy is used to pinpoint an area of space from which strong signals are received. Ordinary telescopes then search this area in order to discover the source of the signals.

Radium is a very rare metal which is extremely radioactive. It gives off intense streams of atomic particles, or radiation. This radiation is widely used in medicine for treating cancer. But in

The giant bowl of the Jodrell Bank radio telescope.

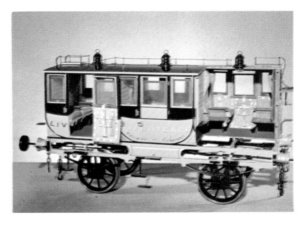

Model of the carriage *Experience*. This carried first class passengers on the Liverpool and Manchester Railway in 1834. Third class carriages of the same period did not have roofs or seats. If it rained, the passengers had to hold up umbrellas to keep dry.

large doses the radiation is very dangerous. Marie Curie, who with her husband Pierre discovered radium in 1898, died of leukaemia caused by constant exposure to radiation.

By giving off radiation from its atoms, radium changes, or *decays,* eventually into lead. Radium itself is formed by the decay of uranium. (See Radioactivity.)

Luminous paints contain traces of radium compounds. The radiation causes chemicals in the paint, such as zinc sulphide, to glow in the dark.

Radnorshire (area 470 square miles), a Welsh county on the border with England, is noted for its sheep breeding. Its county town is Llandrindod Wells, and its population is 18,600.

The county is mostly made up of wild, high moorlands, the highest of which is Radnor Forest, at just over 2,000 feet. These features lend themselves to sheep, cattle and mountain pony breeding. The main rivers are the Teme in the northeast and the Wye in the south. Birmingham draws its water from reservoirs in the Elan valley. Much of the population is scattered among small villages. Llandrindod Wells is a popular spa.

Railways Until the 1700's, transport by land was desperately slow and had changed little for thousands of years. The roads were in a terrible condition, being dust baths in summer and rivers of mud in winter. Travelling by stage-coach was uncomfortable and unreliable, and there was always the problem of highwaymen to contend with.

In the late 1700's several attempts were made to adapt the newly invented steam engine to a road carriage, but they failed because of the state of the roads. But in

Below: Freight containers are helping to speed up the transportation of goods by rail. The containers can be transferred between trucks, railway waggons, and even ships without ever being unloaded.
Bottom: Railway tracks are frequently inspected with the aid of delicate instruments which can detect even the smallest defect in the metal rails.

1803, the British engineer Richard Trevithick hit on the idea of mounting the steam carriage on rails to provide a smoother ride. A year later Trevithick demonstrated the first rail locomotive. The idea of 'rail-ways' was not new, however. Horse-drawn railways, or *tramways*, were being used in most large mines at that time.

The first railway line—the Stockton and Darlington colliery line—was opened in 1825. George Stephenson built the 10-mile line and its first engine, *Locomotion*. He built the first passenger line and the engines for it, too. This line was the Liverpool and Manchester Railway (1830), and the first locomotive to run on it was the famous *Rocket*.

From then on, development was rapid. Lines were opened all over the world, most of them using British locomotives to start with. Some of the finest engineers of the day worked on the railways. One of the greatest was I. K. Brunel, who was

Elaborate signalling systems have been developed to cope with the heavy traffic and high speeds on modern railway systems. In many signal boxes the signalman has only to turn a switch and press a button to change all the points and signals for a train to pass.

in charge of building the Great Western Railway to the West of England. His bridges were engineering masterpieces.

With the growth of the railways, goods and raw materials could be speedily moved between mines and factories, towns and ports. Industrial expansion was rapid. Towns sprang up in previously uninhabited regions. Nowhere was the impact of the railways greater than on the vast continent of North America.

After the American Civil War (1861-5), work started from both sides of the continent on the 'Great American Railway' from the Pacific to the Atlantic coasts. In 1869 the two sections met. The construction of the line was always eventful. If the men were not fighting among themselves, they were fighting off attacks by the Indians, or encountering herds of buffalo. Today, the United States has a greater track mileage than any other country—almost a quarter of a million miles.

Stephenson's locomotives ran on rails that were 4 feet 8½ inches apart. Many countries adopted the same width, or *gauge*, for their railways when they imported British locomotives. Others adopted different gauges. This makes things awkward when the lines of countries with different gauges meet, such as those of France (standard) and Spain (5ft 6in).

Below and right: The monorail is a current development in rail transport. In one design the train is suspended from the single rail. In another design it runs on top of the rail, steadied by wheels on either side as shown in the diagram.

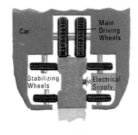

Railways are now being modernized throughout the world in order to meet competition from road and air transport. Electric and diesel locomotives are replacing steam. Branch lines are being closed if they are uneconomic, and main-line services are being speeded up.

Track-laying and maintenance are now highly mechanized. Rails are being welded together to make continuous lengths for smoother running. Built-in automatic warning systems·on the track and in the locomotives help to prevent crashes. Signalling is by swift, push-button control.

At present, railways carry more freight (goods) than passenger traffic. Many goods travel in standard-sized containers, which simplifies handling. There are tanker wagons for bulk liquids, multi-decked transporters for vehicles, and refrigerator·vans for foodstuffs.

Speeds approaching 100 miles an hour are becoming quite usual on some lines. On Japan's New Tokkaido line, the train travels at an *average* speed of over 100

mph. In the future, regular services at over 200 mph may be common. Already, the French *Aérotrain*, which 'hovers' on a single rail (*monorail*), has exceeded 235 mph.

It is probably in monorails, 'hover' trains, and a new method of electric propulsion called *linear induction* that the future of the railways lies.

Rain results from the rising and cooling of moist air. The moisture in the air condenses into water droplets or ice crystals to form clouds (see Condensation). But the cloud particles are a long way from being raindrops, which are about a million times as large. The cloud particles get bigger as they collide with each other or as more moisture condenses on them. Then, when they reach a certain size, they tend to fall towards the ground under their own weight. But they will reach the ground only if they

Below: Map showing annual rainfall throughout the world.

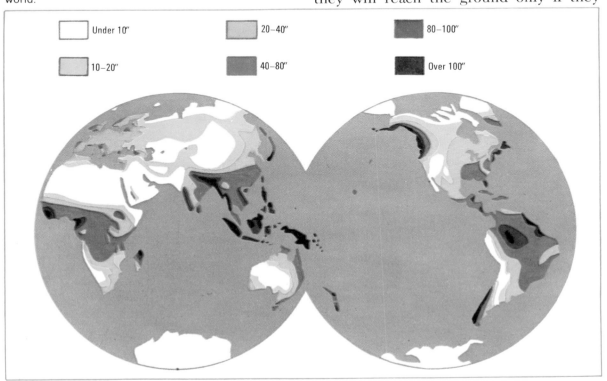

| Under 10″ | 20–40″ | 80–100″ |
| 10–20″ | 40–80″ | Over 100″ |

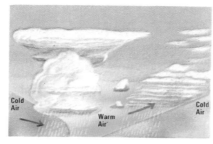

Above: 1. Convectional rain results when heated air rises of its own accord. 2. Orographic rain is caused by air being forced to rise by high land. 3. Frontal rain is caused by warm air meeting cold air and rising over it.

Rain results from the rising and cooling of moist air, and there are a number of ways in which this can happen. A 'parcel' of air will rise of its own accord if it is warmer, and therefore lighter, than the surrounding air. Rain produced in this manner is called *convectional*. Moving air forced to rise to colder levels by high ground lying in its path produces *orographic,* or *relief,* rain. A similar situation occurs when a mass of warm air meets a 'mountain' of cold air. Such masses of air do not mix easily, and the warm air tends to ride up over the ramp of cold air. Rain resulting in this way is called *frontal* or *cyclonic*.

Rainbow Rainbows are caused by the effect of sunlight on countless millions of raindrops. Sunlight is made up of a number of colours which together normally appear as 'white' light. But these colours are separated when sunlight passes through a raindrop and is reflected back from the inside surface. Each colour — red, orange, yellow, green, blue, indigo,

are heavy enough to overcome the resistance of the upward air currents from the surface of the Earth.

Most rain is probably formed from the ice-crystal particles. Whether a cloud consists mainly of water droplets or of ice crystals depends on the temperature. Any part of a cloud with a temperature below about $-40°$ C. $(-40°$ F.) consists entirely of ice crystals. When the ice crystals grow sufficiently heavy, they fall through the cloud, becoming larger as water droplets freeze onto them. Passing through warmer air at lower levels, they melt and fall as raindrops (or, if the temperature is low enough, as snowflakes), perhaps a tenth of an inch across.

Left: A rainbow is made by sunlight shining through tiny drops of water in the air. The raindrop breaks the sunlight up into the colours of which it is formed.
Below: Spectacular rainbows can often be seen in the spray of a waterfall.

violet—comes out at a different angle. A fainter rainbow can usually be seen above the main bow. It is formed by light reflected twice inside the raindrops, and its colours are in the reverse order.

Rainbows occur whenever the Sun shines on rain. But you can see them only if you are between the Sun and the rain, and if the Sun is not too high in the sky. If the Sun is near the horizon, a person in an aircraft or standing on a high hill might be able to see the full circle of the rainbow. The Moon also forms a rainbow, but it is feeble compared with the Sun's, as the Moon's light is only reflected sunlight.

Raleigh, Sir Walter (1552?-1618), was an English soldier and adventurer. Apart from his expeditions against the Spaniards and in the Americas, he introduced tobacco smoking to Europe and brought the potato plant to Ireland.

In 1578, Raleigh undertook an unsuccessful expedition to the Americas with his half-brother Sir Humphrey Gilbert. After a ruthless campaign in Ireland as an army captain, he was sent to the court of Queen Elizabeth. He soon became the queen's favourite, and he was knighted in 1584.

Raleigh tried many times to establish a colony in America, but did not sail with the expeditions which set out to do so. He helped to defeat the Spanish Armada in 1588.

Raleigh angered the queen and lost his influence when he married one of her maids-of-honour. He tried to recover his position by leading an expedition to Guiana in South America to look for the legendary land of *El Dorado*, but the expedition failed.

Elizabeth died in 1603. Raleigh was accused of treason by the new king, James I, and was condemned to death. After a last-minute reprieve Raleigh was imprisoned in the Tower of London. He lived there for twelve years with his wife and son, and wrote his unfinished *History*

Above: Sir Walter Raleigh, who introduced tobacco to Europe, is the unsuspecting victim of his conscientious servant who attempts to 'extinguish' him.
Left: This famous portrait of Sir Walter hangs in the National Portrait Gallery in London.

of the World. In 1616 he was freed to lead his last expedition. He went to South America in search of gold. Some of his men attacked the Spaniards there, and Raleigh returned to England where he was executed for disobeying orders.

Ranching is the practice of rearing and caring for great herds of cattle or flocks of sheep on large farms. It is very important in North, Central and South America, Australia and New Zealand, and southern Africa. In Canada and the United States, the farms are called *ranches,* and in Spanish-speaking countries such as Argentina and Mexico, they are called *haciendas.* In Australia and New Zealand, large sheep farms are called *sheep stations.* The farms may be very large. In the United States, a ranch is usually about 10,000 to 20,000 acres in size. But some ranches have an area of 100,000 acres.

In these countries, the farms are generally privately owned. The owner employs many hands to look after the herds

When cattle grazed on the grass and scrub of the open range the whole year round, a ranch of 150 square miles in the U.S.A. could support only a few thousand head of cattle during the winter. Now the cattle are brought in to enclosed pastures for winter feeding.

or flocks on the great expanses of grazing land. Large cattle and sheep farms usually grow grass as a crop to feed their animals during the winter. Large *collective* cattle and sheep farms exist in communist countries, especially Russia. The farms are owned by the state and managed by a group of farmers.

In the United States, people refer to most large farms as ranches, even if they produce fruit or different animals. A *dude ranch* is a kind of holiday camp built like an old Wild West ranch.

Raphael (1483-1520) was a great Italian painter of the Renaissance—the rebirth of learning and the arts that took place from the 1300's to the 1500's. His full name was Raffaello Sanzio.

Raphael was born in Urbino, in northeastern Italy. His first art lessons were given to him by his father. Later he studied with the great master Perugino. At 21, Raphael went to Florence to study the works of Leonardo da Vinci, Fra Bartolommeo and other famous painters. During this period he painted many pictures of the Madonna (the Virgin Mary). They are known for their gentleness and beauty. When Raphael was 25, Pope Julius II asked him to come to Rome to decorate rooms in the Vatican. Two of his best-known Vatican paintings are the *School of Athens* and the *Disputa*. Both are frescoes—pictures painted on a wall while the plaster was still wet. While at the Vatican, Raphael met Michelangelo. From him he learned much about painting the human figure. Raphael's work at the Vatican added to his growing fame. He soon had a large studio, and had assistants working under him.

Besides being a great painter, Raphael was also an architect. He was for a time the chief architect of St. Peter's Basilica in Rome. He also designed many beautiful tapestries. Raphael died when he was 37.

Rat The rat is one of the group of mammals called *rodents* (see Rodent). It is closely related to mice, but is much larger (see Mouse). The black rat grows to a length of about 16 inches, half of which is the naked tail. The brown rat is even bigger, but has a shorter tail and ears. Both have spread to almost every part of the world. They are pests, doing great damage to food supplies and buildings, and spreading diseases. Both—but particularly the black rat—often infest ships' holds: The brown rat is more common in country areas than the black rat. Specially bred white rats are used in medical research.

Rayon is a silky, lustrous fibre made from cellulose from wood-pulp or cotton. The most common kinds of rayon are *viscose* and *triacetate*. Triacetate rayons are better known under their trade names of Arnel (United States) and Tricel (Britain).

Viscose rayon is one of the most widely used of all textile fibres. In long, filament form it is used to make the corded fabric in automobile tyres. In short, staple form it is spun into yarn for use in all kinds of clothing and especially for carpets. Triacetate fabrics can be permanently pleated.

Viscose is made up of pure cellulose, which has been dissolved and then re-formed, or *regenerated* from solution in fibre form. (See Fibres.) Triacetate is a compound of cellulose which has been made into fibres in a similar way.

Recording Until 1877, no-one had heard the sound of his own voice as others hear it. But in that year the American inventor Thomas Alva Edison built a machine that recorded sound. He called it a *phonograph*, which means 'sound writer'. And that is what it was. A needle, vibrated by the voice, cut a wavy groove in a piece of

The *Vision of a Knight* is one of the beautiful paintings by Raphael at the National Gallery, London, England.

tin foil on a revolving cylinder. Putting the needle back in the groove on the cylinder reproduced the original sound. In 1885, two other American inventors, C. A. Bell and C. S. Tainter produced the *Graphophone,* which used a cylinder coated with wax instead of tin foil. Two years later Emile Berliner, a German, invented the *Gramophone* which played a flat wax disc instead of a cylinder.

Our modern record player developed from the phonograph. Now, of course, recording and playing back is done electrically. But it still depends on the same principle of a wavy groove and a vibrating needle.

We now have other methods of recording sound, such as the tape-recorder, in which sounds are recorded on magnetic tape. The sound for films is recorded as a varying pattern of light on the same strip of film as the pictures. (See Cinema.)

The making of the discs we play on our record-player takes quite a long time. Most recordings, say, of music are made in a recording studio, which is like a miniature concert hall. *Microphones* placed at various points in the studio pick up the sounds to be recorded. In the microphone, the sounds are changed into a variable electric current. This goes to a tape-recorder which records it as a magnetic 'pattern' on tape.

To cut the record disc, the finished tape is played back in a tape-recorder. The electrical signals produced go to a sharp cutting *stylus,* or needle, and make it vibrate from side to side. The stylus cuts wavy grooves in a rotating lacquered aluminium disc, called the *master.* This is electroplated with copper, and then moulds are made from it. The finished disc is produced by pressing a piece of plastic into the mould.

To reproduce the sound, we put the disc on the turntable of a record player, and play it at the same speed at which it was recorded—78, 45, or $33\frac{1}{3}$ revolutions per minute. The needle, or stylus, in the *pick-up head* vibrates in the groove.

The vibrations are changed in the head to a variable electric current, which is identical to that originally produced in the microphone of the recording studio. The current is strengthened in an *amplifier* before going to a *loudspeaker* which converts it into sound.

The recorded music can be made to sound more realistic by using pairs of microphones for recording and a pair of loudspeakers for playing back. The microphones are placed to the right and left of the performer, and the speakers are placed to the right and left of the listener. Each side of the record's groove feeds 'right' and 'left' signals to the right and left speakers. This produces an 'all-round', or *stereophonic* sound which is similar to that of a live performance.

Tape-recording is something we can do ourselves quite easily. The operation and control of a tape-recorder simply involve pressing a few buttons. We can record through a microphone or directly from a radio or record player. They all produce variable electrical signals which are fed into the *recording head* of the recorder. There the electric signals are changed into a variable magnetic field.

The tape is wound past the head from one reel to the other. It consists of a plastic strip coated with magnetized particles. As it passes the head, the particles are arranged in patterns corresponding to the variable magnetic field.

Playing back is the reverse of recording. A *play-back head* 'reads' the patterns on the tape and converts them to electric signals. These are fed to a loudspeaker, which reproduces the original sounds.

Sound is not the only thing that can be recorded on magnetic tape. Television pictures can be, too. They are recorded on a very wide tape, called *video tape.* In the television camera, a picture is converted into electric signals. And it is these signals which can be recorded.

Red Cross This world-wide organization was founded in the late 1800's to aid

In Edison's 'improved phonograph', a needle, vibrated by the voice, cut a wavy groove in wax on a revolving cylinder. Putting the needle back into the groove on the cylinder reproduced the original sound. Modern record players developed from the phonograph.

A film sound track is put on the side of a film to ensure that the sound is synchronized with the vision. In the variable density sound track (top) the sound is converted to varying electrical signals which are used to produce a similarly varying series of grey and black stripes. These can be used to reproduce the original sound. In the variable width sound track (bottom) the electrical signals are converted into a continuous black band of varying thickness which can be used to reproduce the original sound.

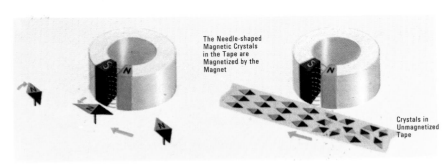

The Needle-shaped Magnetic Crystals in the Tape are Magnetized by the Magnet

Crystals in Unmagnetized Tape

Left: In tape recording, sound is converted to varying electrical signals and then to a varying magnetic field. This impresses a pattern on the tape coated with magnetized particles which is passed by the recording head. Playing back is the reverse of recording.

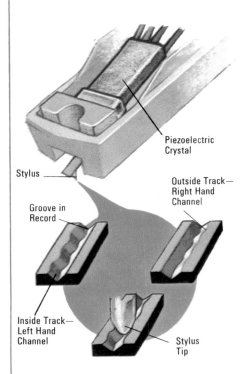

Piezoelectric Crystal

Stylus

Groove in Record

Outside Track— Right Hand Channel

Inside Track— Left Hand Channel

Stylus Tip

Recorded music can be made to sound more realistic by using pairs of microphones for recording and a pair of loudspeakers for playing back. The microphones are placed to the right and left of the performer, and the speakers are placed to the right and left of the listener. Each side of the record's groove feeds 'right' and 'left' signals to the right and left speakers. This produces an 'all-round', or stereophonic sound which is similar to that of a live performance.

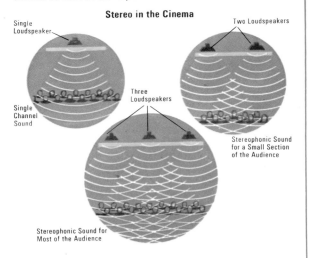

Stereo in the Cinema

Single Loudspeaker

Two Loudspeakers

Single Channel Sound

Three Loudspeakers

Stereophonic Sound for a Small Section of the Audience

Stereophonic Sound for Most of the Audience

soldiers wounded in battle. Since that time it has greatly extended its activities to help all people who are suffering, in peace as well as in war.

There is hardly any sphere where medical and other help is needed, such as disasters, accidents, disease, or disablement, where the Red Cross organization is not found in the forefront of work to relieve suffering and need. This great society was formed as a result of the ideals and activity of Henri Dunant, a young Swiss banker. In 1859 he visited northern Italy, and was in the town of Castiglione when the French were fighting the Austrians, at the Battle of Solferino. Dunant was appalled by what he saw. After the battle more than 40,000 men lay dead or wounded, with hardly anyone to care for the wounded.

Dunant turned the town of Castiglione into one vast hospital, and organized what help he could get to relieve the suffering. Without knowledge and medical supplies, there was comparatively little that Dunant and his helpers could do, but they felt that anything was better than nothing.

This wonderful spirit has inspired the Red Cross workers ever since, though nowadays they are well organized and equipped. Dunant's ideal was to realize that all men are brothers and need the help of one another in adversity.

On his return to Switzerland he campaigned for a universal recognition of the need to relieve suffering. As a result of his activities the great Geneva Convention was drawn up. This laid down a code of conduct for dealing with wounded people, and prisoners of war, and eventually many nations agreed to be bound by its provisions. The Geneva Convention has been revised and extended to cover the widest aspects of the suffering of prisoners and wounded since then. The Swiss, who are always neutral in wars, are accepted by all people as administrators of the Red Cross code. Today, the Red Cross has many branches in all parts of the world, although it is known as the *Red Crescent*, or the

1106

Red Lion or *Sun*, in some Muslim countries.

Red Sea This is an arm of the Indian Ocean that separates north-eastern Africa from the Arabian Peninsula. It is about 2,400 miles long and between 100 and 220 miles wide.

It may get its name from the tiny sea creatures that tinge its waters red, or from the reddish colour of its shores. The Israelites escaped from the Pharaoh of Egypt across the Red Sea, according to the Bible.

Reformation Protestant Churches today have their origins in a split in the Catholic Church which took place in the sixteenth century. This split is called the Reformation. A German friar called Martin Luther (1483-1546) was the man who, almost accidentally, started this great change. Luther believed that the leaders of the Church were corrupt and not fit to lead the Christian faith. He wrote a document called the 95 *theses* in which he attacked the sale of *indulgencies*. These were written 'pardons' and people who bought them were promised a reduction in the amount of time that they would have to spend in purgatory. He pinned the 95 theses to the door of Wittenberg Cathedral in 1517. As a result of this attack on the leaders of the Church, the Pope excommunicated Luther (expelled him from the Church) and the Emperor of Germany made him an outlaw.

But Luther's overlord, the Elector of Saxony, protected him and allowed him to bring in the changes he thought necessary in the Church organization and services. Services were now held in German instead of Latin. Luther translated the Bible and wrote a number of hymns for the congregations to sing. Luther no longer accepted the Pope as Head of the Church. He believed that the leaders of

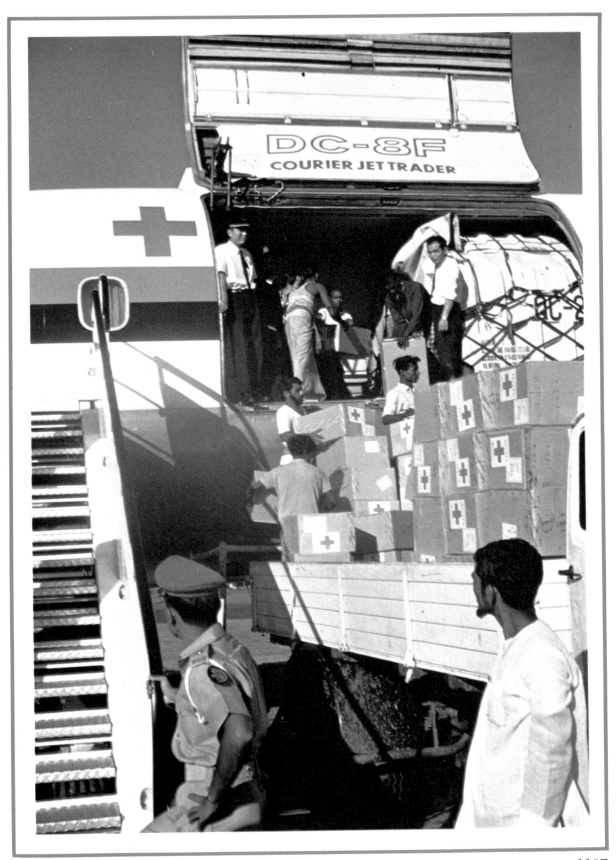

Right: Martin Luther was an Augustinian friar and university teacher. In 1517, disgusted by the apparent corruption of the Catholic Church, he pinned his revolutionary '95 theses' to the cathedral door in Wittenberg and sparked off a dispute that led to the Reformation and to the establishment of Protestant Churches.

Although many English people were dissatisfied with the Church, and sympathised with Luther, in Germany, the Reformation in England was not brought about solely for religious reasons. The main cause of it was political. In 1526 Henry VIII (above left) wanted to divorce his wife in order to remarry. To do this he was forced to break with Rome. He declared himself head of the Church in England and although he was a devout Catholic, he persecuted people in England who opposed his will. His friend Sir Thomas More (above right) could not sanction the divorce and resigned his position as Lord Chancellor. When he refused to take the oath of supremacy he was imprisoned in the Tower of London and later tried for treason. In 1535 he was beheaded.

the Catholic Church were evil, rich and lazy and were not fit to guide and advise other Christians. His ideas spread widely and his reforms were copied in many parts of Germany.

Some German rulers supported Luther because they disliked paying money to the Pope, and they wanted an excuse to rebel against the Emperor. A number of princes and cities signed a 'Protest' in which they declared their belief in these new religious ideas. As a result, followers of Luther were called Protestants. The word came to be applied to all those who split away from the Catholic Church.

In Switzerland Ulrich Zwingli carried Protestant ideas a good deal further than Luther. In Geneva a Frenchman called John Calvin reformed the Church, and the clergy came to play an important part in running the city. Many modern Protestant Churches, the Presbyterian and Baptist Churches for example, grew up as a result of Calvin's work.

These changes were not always peaceful. In Germany, Switzerland and France in the middle and late sixteenth century terrible religious wars were fought between Catholics and Protestants, before men of different beliefs learned to live together.

Refrigerator We can keep food fresh for a time by cooling it in a refrigerator. Cooling slows down the processes which cause food to spoil.

Refrigerators work on the principle that a liquid absorbs heat when it *vaporizes*, or turns into a gas. In a refrigerator, a substance called a *refrigerant* is circulated through coils in the food compartment and made to turn into gas there. As it does so, it takes up heat from the food. The gas is then changed back into a liquid and recirculated.

Gas and electric refrigerators differ in the way in which the refrigerant is changed back from gas to liquid. Gas refrigerators work on a complicated *absorption* system. Electric refrigerators work on a simpler *compression* system.

Refuse disposal is very important if our homes, streets, towns and villages are to be pleasant and healthy places in which to live. Every day, the sanitation departments of local governments have to get rid of thousands of tons of tin cans, bottles, paper, unwanted food, rags, old furniture and other things that people throw away. In many countries, each person throws away 700 or more pounds of refuse a year.

Because the number of people in the world is increasing, the amount of refuse is also increasing. People today have more possessions than people had in the past. When these possessions become old or are not needed any longer, they are thrown away. But even new goods are a major source of refuse, because they are generally wrapped in paper or packaged in some other way. The packaging is thrown away immediately after the goods are used.

In the past, people simply tipped their rubbish somewhere, or threw it into the sea or a river. In the Middle Ages, people

Below: The vapour compression refrigerator. Refrigerant vapour is compressed (A), then cooled by the surrounding air so that it liquefies (B). The liquid escapes through an expansion valve (C) and becomes a cold vapour which takes up heat from the food compartment (D). Bottom: The gas absorption refrigerator. Ammonia, the refrigerant, is heated in the generator. Vapour is driven off and liquefied by the condenser. The cold liquid passes to the evaporator where it vaporizes and takes up heat from the food compartment. In the absorber the ammonia dissolves in water forming a concentrated solution. Some of the weak solution left in the generator is siphoned into it and the resulting solution passes to the generator for the process to begin again.

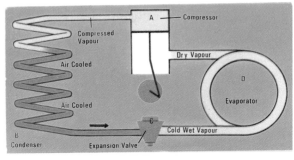

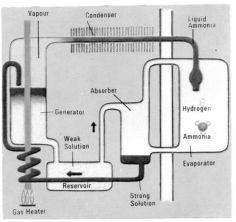

Refuse is collected by a local government employee.

in towns threw their refuse into the street. These habits polluted water and made streets and other places unsightly, smelly and dirty. They also spread disease, because of the rats, flies and germs that lived in the heaps of rotting food and rags.

Most households today have large metal or plastic dustbins for refuse. The bins have tight lids to keep out animals and flies. Dustmen with special refuse vehicles empty these dustbins at least once a week. A mechanism in the vehicles cuts up and crushes the rubbish so that it takes up a minimum of space. The vehicles are then emptied at refuse disposal sites, where the refuse is tipped into wide pits and covered with soil. Sometimes, disposal sites are located in marshy areas. Gradually the marshy land is filled in by the rubbish tipped on to it and is *reclaimed* (made usable) for building.

Some towns dispose of refuse by *incinerating* (burning) it in large furnaces. The ash and clinkers can be used for reclaiming marshy areas, or can simply be buried. But incineration has a serious drawback. It pours harmful smoke and ashes into the air. Towns may also dispose of refuse by treating it with chemicals. One chemical process removes the grease for factory use, and converts the remainder into fertilizer. Researchers are working to develop other processes.

In some communities, people have electric waste disposal units in their sinks. These units grind or liquefy refuse and send it into the sewers. But such systems can only be used where the sewers are equipped to deal with the extra material coming into them.

Reindeer The reindeer is a thick-coated deer of the cold northern parts of Asia and Europe. It is closely related to the caribou which lives in North America. The male reindeer stands up to 4 feet high at the shoulder, but the caribou is larger. Unlike other types of deer, the female reindeer has antlers as well as the male. Those of the male are magnificent, branching and sweeping back, then upwards and forwards. They may grow to 5 feet in length. In northern Europe and Asia, reindeer have been domesticated for centuries. They provide meat and milk, and skins for clothing.

Relativity In 1905, Albert Einstein put forward his special theory of relativity. It concerns, among other things, the effect of motion on time, length, and mass. For instance the theory predicts that in a space-ship hurtling across the Universe at nearly the speed of light, time would pass more slowly, the ship's length would become smaller, and its mass would become larger than on a similar space-ship stationary on Earth.

The effects are due to the *relative* motion of the space-ship and the Earth. If you are travelling along in a car at 40 miles an hour and you are overtaken by a car travelling at 60 miles an hour, the second car appears to pull away from you at 20 miles an hour. Its true speed, *relative* to the ground is 60 miles an hour, but its speed *relative* to you is 20 miles an hour.

Another important result of the special theory is the famous equation $E = mc^2$, which shows the equivalence of energy and mass. For instance, it predicted the tremendous amounts of energy released in atomic and hydrogen bombs. In 1915, Einstein put forward the general theory of relativity which deals mainly with gravity and acceleration.

Religions are organized systems of belief in one or more gods and in certain ways of life. Many religions try to explain the creation of the world and of mankind and contain the belief in another existence after death.

Primitive man worshipped simple things such as stones, the Sun, or a river. Some tribal groups in places such as Africa still worship sacred carved poles (totems). Primitive man endowed objects with superhuman powers by worshipping fetishes. A *fetish* is an object or animal containing a magic spirit which can ward off evil and danger. Gradually the belief in these magical powers led to the creation of gods. The cult of the dead was also widespread, as we can see from the preserved remains of ancient Egyptian tombs. Most early religions had special festivals

Left: A young Muslim kneels and bows his head to the ground as he prays to Allah. Muslim men must always face Mecca, the birthplace of Mohammed, when they pray, and remove their shoes before entering the mosque.

Left: Christianity has spread all over the world as a result of active missionary work. Here an Anglican minister, clothed in ornate vestments, holds the Easter service in Accra.

Below left: Buddhist monks, in their saffron robes, stand before a 'reclining' Buddha in a Thai temple.

Below right: The River Ganges is regarded as sacred by the Hindus. Hindu pilgrims bathe and drink the water off the steps (ghats) which line the waterfront.

and sacrificial rites, and the first laws of society probably sprang from *taboos* (prohibitions).

We give the term *Animism* to the belief of some primitive peoples that inanimate objects possess spirits of their own. Later, *Pantheism* spread, especially among Hindu peoples. This is the belief that God exists everywhere and all things are divine.

Important world religions of today can be divided into three main types. *Monotheism,* or belief in one supreme god, as illustrated by Christianity, Judaism and Islam; *polytheism,* or the worship of several gods, as found in Hinduism; and *dualism,* the belief in equal forces of good and evil, as in the religion of Zoroastrianism.

Christianity has almost 1,000 million adherents. It is the religion professed by the followers of Jesus Christ, whose teachings are found in the New Testament. Judaism, one of the oldest monotheistic religions, has its centre in Palestine, but the 13 million Jews are scattered throughout the world. There are about 479 million Muslims, 365 million followers of Confucius, 417 million Hindus, and at least 170 million Buddhists. Other important world faiths include Bahaism, Jainism, Taoism, Sikhism and Zoroastrianism.

There are several minority religions and also people who do not subscribe to any religion who are called *atheists* (people who reject religion and belief in a god) and *agnostics* (people who do not know whether to believe or not). (See Buddhism; Christianity; Confucius; Hinduism; Islam; Judaism.)

Rembrandt (1606-1669) was one of the most famous artists who ever lived, and also one of the most hard-working. He painted at least 600 paintings, made several thousands of drawings, and many etchings. His full name was Rembrandt

Hermenszoon van Rijn, and he was born at Leyden, in the Netherlands. His father wanted him to enter some learned profession, but he was determined to become a painter, and by the time he was 20, was already making a name for himself. He was particularly fascinated by effects of light and shade, and liked to paint naturalistic scenes of ordinary life. In his sketchbook were drawings ranging from a grandfather teaching his grandson to walk, to those of an old tramp sunning himself. However, he also did religious paintings, landscapes, and many portraits of himself and his family. In 1632 Rembrandt's fame was growing. He moved to Amsterdam, and became a favourite portrait painter there. His first great picture, *The Anatomy Lesson,* was painted at this time. It portrays his friend, Dr Tulp, lecturing to other doctors.

Rembrandt exhibits in his portraits a deep knowledge of human nature. The thoughts and feelings behind each face, whether his own or someone else's, are clearly revealed.
Left: 'The Painter in Later Age'.
Below: 'Jewish Merchant'.

In 1634 he married Saskia van Uylenborch, and they had one son, Titus. Rembrandt painted several beautiful portraits of his wife and son. From the time of his marriage until 1641, he was prosperous and popular. He bought a large house which he filled with works of art.

In 1641 the Civic Guards of Amsterdam asked him to paint a portrait of their company on parade. They expected a straight-forward group, but Rembrandt produced a wonderfully natural and lively painting, full of light and shade, showing up their richly coloured uniforms. The Civic Guards were very annoyed because their faces were half-hidden and indistinct. Rembrandt refused to alter the painting into a conventional group, and he became less popular, and began to lose money. To add to his troubles, his wife died in 1642, and he was forced to sell his house and treasures. His servant, Hendrickje Stoffels, who had looked after him since his wife died, set up an art dealer's business with Rembrandt's son. With their help he was able to continue painting until the early 1660's, when his sight began to fail.

Renaissance means 'rebirth'. The Renaissance began as a revival of the art and ideas of Greece and Rome. It took place between 1300 and 1600, first in Italy and then spreading slowly northwards. Scholars began to learn Greek so that they could read the plays and philosophy of Aeschylus and Plato. Universities began to teach the language to their students. From these studies people gained a new attitude to life. They were more curious about things around them and about other people. They began to experiment and try out new ideas.

Italian writers, such as Dante (1264-1321) and Petrarch (1304-1374), wrote poetry in their own language. Previously Latin was considered the only suitable language for such work.

Architects started to build palaces (Doges' palace, Venice) and cathedrals

Above: Erasmus, the Dutch humanist and intellectual, was one of the greatest Renaissance scholars.
Right: Brunelleschi's famous dome in Florence probably served as a model for St Peter's in Rome.

(Milan, Florence) more like buildings of ancient Greece and Rome.

Sculptors and artists became more expert. They went to hospitals to study anatomy so that their figures would look life-like. They also studied the laws of perspective to give their paintings 'depth'. New subjects were thought worth painting. Before the Renaissance, nearly all paintings were made to beautify the walls of churches. Their subjects were taken from Bible stories. Now artists drew on the legends of Greece; they painted portraits of real people. Nothing was too small or too unimportant to paint. A German artist called Dürer (1471-1528) made beautiful studies of a hare and of wild plants. The Flemish painter Pieter Brueghel (1525-1569) painted homely scenes of village life.

The artists and sculptors of the Renaissance usually worked for rich men who were their patrons. Such men wanted to be famous after their death. The Medici, the most powerful family in Florence, ordered from Gozzoli (1420-1497) a painting showing the journey of the Wise Men. In this picture we can identify most of the famous men of Florence at that time, including the artist himself. Pope Julius II (1503-1513) persuaded the great sculptor Michelangelo (1475-1564) to design and make his tomb. This artist, together with Leonardo da Vinci (1452-1519) and Raphael (1483-1520), are considered to be the three greatest artists of this wonderful period.

Renfrewshire (area 225 square miles) a county of west central Scotland, lies on the south bank of the Clyde estuary. Its county town is Renfrew, and its population is 362,100.

The county is mainly low-lying, although there are some high moorlands and hills in the west and south-west. The principal rivers are the White, Black Cart and Gryfe. *Lochs* (lakes) in the hills supply water for the lowland towns.

Below: Renaissance painters, such as Titian, brought a new realism to religious subjects.

1113

Oats, potatoes and turnips are cultivated, and there are many small dairy farms. Cotton and flax spinning and woollen manufacture are major industries. Paisley is the administrative centre. Most of the people and the factories are found in the north, in the region round Greenock, Gourock and Port Glasgow on the Clyde estuary.

Reproduction is the process by which plants and animals make new organisms like themselves. It is a basic process of life. It is not essential for an individual creature's survival, but it is vital for the survival of the *species* (kind).

Some animals and plants can reproduce on their own, simply by dividing in two or by producing small parts that develop into complete new organisms. This is called *asexual* reproduction. Other organisms reproduce *sexually*. They produce special cells called *gametes*. When a gamete from a male organism *fertilizes* (joins with) a gamete from a female, they form a *zygote*, which develops into a new individual.

The simplest animals reproduce asexually. So do many plants, even those that can also reproduce sexually. The one-celled amoeba reproduces by fission (dividing in two). First, the nucleus—the creature's control centre—divides. Then the rest of the cell splits.

Many non-flowering plants (such as fungi) reproduce asexually by producing *spores*, tiny seed-like cells that later develop into new plants. Asexual reproduction is common in flowering plants. It occurs when a gardener divides a daffodil bulb or a seed potato (a tuber) in two, when he plants strawberry runners, or when he takes a cutting from a rose tree. In each case, part of the plant splits off and develops into a complete new plant. This kind of reproduction is also called *vegetative reproduction*.

Flowering plants also reproduce sexually by means of flowers and seeds. In some plants, the male and female flowers are on separate plants; in some they are on different parts of the same plant; while in others they form different parts of the same flower. The *stamens* produce pollen grains, which carry the male gametes. The *pistil* is the female part of the flower, and contains egg cells (female gametes). When pollen is carried to the pistil, fertilization takes place and the egg cell develops into a seed. This grows into a new plant.

All but the simplest animals reproduce sexually. The male gametes are called *sperms*; the female gametes are called *eggs*. Most female fishes lay their eggs in the water. The male, swimming behind, deposits his sperms on them. This is wasteful, because many sperms are lost and many eggs are not fertilized. After fertilization, the *embryo* (developing) fish grows while using the store of food contained in the egg.

Frogs reproduce in a similar way to fish, but in most higher animals fertilization takes place inside the female's body. After fertilization the female reptile or bird lays her eggs, which are protected by shells. The embryo develops inside the shell, using the food stored inside, until it is ready to hatch.

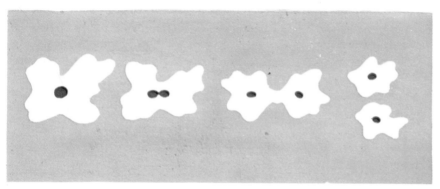

The one-celled amoeba reproduces by dividing in two. First the nucleus divides, and then the rest of the cell.

In mammals, fertilization also takes place inside the female, but she does not lay her eggs. Instead, the embryo develops inside its mother until it is ready to be born. During this period of *gestation*, the embryo receives food from its mother's bloodstream. She also feeds it — with milk — after birth. An embryo mammal has far better protection inside its mother than do the embryos of egg-laying creatures.

Reptiles are the class of animals that includes lizards and snakes, crocodiles and alligators, and turtles. Reptiles evolved from amphibians about 250 million years ago. They differ from amphibians in that their skin is scaly and the young are born resembling their parents.

From the time of their appearance on the Earth to about 70 million years ago, reptiles dominated the land. Some, the *dinosaurs,* grew to a great size. Others, the *pterosaurs,* flew in the air. But these creatures died out suddenly. Today, reptiles live on land and in water, and some, such as the giant crocodiles and snakes, grow as large as 30 feet. The smallest reptiles are lizards about two inches long.

Reptiles are cold-blooded animals — their body temperature is the same as the temperature of their surroundings. For this reason, reptiles are not found in polar regions, where they would become too cold to survive. In tropical regions, they can often be seen sunning themselves, and then moving into the shade when they become too hot. In regions with a cold winter, reptiles hibernate. Most reptiles lay eggs, but a few bear living young.

There are four main groups or *orders* of living reptiles: the crocodiles and alligators; the turtles, tortoises, and terrapins; the lizards and snakes; and the tuatara.

Crocodiles and alligators make up the order *Crocodilia*. This order also includes the caymans and gavials. They are all large animals with cigar-shaped bodies and

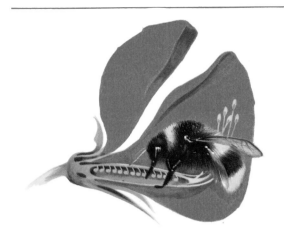

Plants reproduce either sexually or asexually. Above: The bee often acts as the agent of sexual reproduction, by depositing pollen from one flower on the pistil of another. Left: Rose trees reproduce asexually by growing *suckers* from their roots.

long, powerful tails. Their jaws are lined with rows of sharp teeth. They live in fresh water or salt water in tropical regions around the world, feeding on animals such as fish, birds, and small mammals. (See Crocodiles and Alligators.)

Turtles, tortoises, and terrapins make up the order *Chelonia*. The use of these names varies from country to country. What some call a tortoise or terrapin, others may call a turtle. But they all have two protecting shells, between which four legs and a head protrude. They live in fresh and salt water and on land in the warmer regions of the world. Most of the land animals eat only plants, whereas the aquatic animals are generally carnivorous (flesh-eating). (See Tortoise and Turtles.)

Lizards and snakes form the order *Squamata*. Most lizards have four legs, whereas snakes have no legs. They differ from snakes in that they have movable

1115

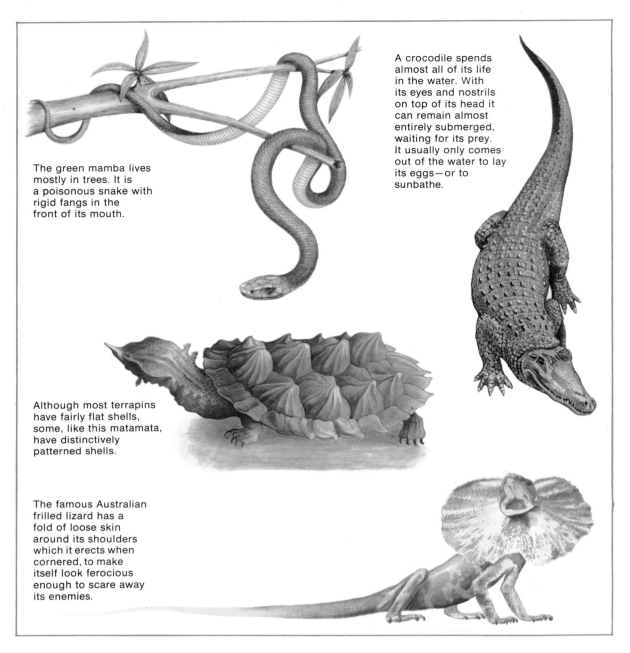

The green mamba lives mostly in trees. It is a poisonous snake with rigid fangs in the front of its mouth.

A crocodile spends almost all of its life in the water. With its eyes and nostrils on top of its head it can remain almost entirely submerged, waiting for its prey. It usually only comes out of the water to lay its eggs—or to sunbathe.

Although most terrapins have fairly flat shells, some, like this matamata, have distinctively patterned shells.

The famous Australian frilled lizard has a fold of loose skin around its shoulders which it erects when cornered, to make itself look ferocious enough to scare away its enemies.

eyelids and external ears. And they do not possess the snake's deeply forked tongue. Lizards and snakes are found in temperate as well as warm regions. They vary greatly in size and range from lizards of two inches long to snakes of 30 feet. (See Lizards; Slow Worm; Snakes.)

The tuatara resembles a spiny lizard, but the structure of its skull is different from that of a lizard. It is two feet long, and lives on a few islands off the coast of New Zealand. The remarkable thing about the tuatara is that it is the only surviving member of the order *Rhynchocephalia*, which originated about 200 million years ago.

Rhine The Rhine, a river in Europe, flows 800 miles from its source to the North Sea. It rises in the mountains of Switzerland, near Lake Constance. It flows north through France and Germany, then west to the sea through the Netherlands.

The Rhine has been a great highway

of commerce for centuries, and still is. It is linked by a wonderful system of canals to the French river system and to the Weser and Elbe rivers of northern Germany.

The middle course of the Rhine is a region of wooded hills and fertile valleys, widening into a great plain. Wheat and vines are the main crops grown on the highly cultivated farmland, which is mainly divided into smallholdings of five to ten acres.

Industry has grown rapidly in the Rhine Valley, and Cologne has become one of the most important railway centres in Europe. The Rhine is navigable by river barges as high up as Basle, while the great seaports of Hamburg and Bremen can be reached by canal.

The region is rich in coal, iron ore, and potash. The production of iron and steel is enormous, and heavy industrial machinery, automobiles and electrical goods are manufactured. Chemicals, dyes and textiles are other important industries.

For centuries, the Rhine has been an important frontier between the peoples to the east who spoke German, and those to the west who did not.

Rhinoceros This is a huge, ungainly mammal that has—depending on the kind—one or two thick horns growing upwards from its snout. The black rhinoceros and white rhinoceros of Africa and the very rare Sumatran rhinoceros of Asia have two horns, one behind the other, the front horn generally being the longer. The Javan rhinoceros and Indian rhinoceros of Asia have single horns. All rhinoceros' horns are hard outgrowths from the skin and have no bony core. They are not true horns (see Horns and antlers).

The white rhinoceros (which is grey rather than white) is the third biggest land animal in the world, and may weigh more than three tons and stand six feet high at the shoulder. The other kinds are

In the Rhine gorge terraced hillsides covered in vineyards stretch for miles, and small picturesque towns nestle by the banks.

Left: The rhinoceros is a ferocious animal. Because of its poor sight it is liable to charge at any moving object.

Right: Cecil Rhodes bequeathed most of the vast fortune he amassed from the diamond fields of Africa, for the provision of student scholarships to Oxford University.

smaller, but all have massive bodies and thick, short legs. Their thick, hard skin hangs in folds. They live mainly in grasslands, eating only plant food.

Rhode Island, in New England, is the smallest state in the United States. It is known as 'Little Rhodie'. It covers an area of only 1,214 square miles, but with almost 950,000 people, it is one of the most densely populated states. Rhode Island borders the Atlantic Ocean. Narragansett Bay cuts deeply into it, creating a mainland area and 36 islands. The state once had thriving whaling and ship-building industries and carried on a busy shipping trade. Today, fishing is still important. During the summer, yachting is popular.

Rhode Island has a number of important naval bases. More than half the state is forested, and farming, principally dairying and poultry farming, is a minor industry.

Location map of Rhode Island. It is the smallest yet one of the most densely populated states in the U.S.A.

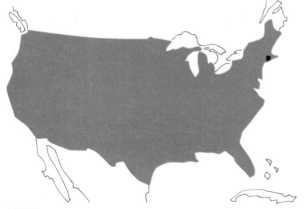

Most of its wealth comes from textile milling, machinery manufacture and the production of jewellery and silver-ware. Providence is the capital and the most important town. Nearby Warwick and Cranston are industrial centres.

European explorers visited Rhode Island in 1524 and 1614. In 1636, Roger Williams, with other English colonists from Massachusetts who were seeking religious and political freedom, founded Providence settlement. Other settlements followed, and in 1663, Rhode Island became a British colony. Rhode Island was the last of the 13 original colonies to become a state.

Rhodes, Cecil John (1853-1902), was an Englishman who became a South African statesman. He created a new British colony in Africa, and used his immense wealth to enlarge the British Empire.

When Rhodes was 17 he went to Natal, then a British colony in South Africa. He soon found himself in Kimberley, prospecting for diamonds. He bought claims from other diggers and eventually gained complete control of the diamond fields.

He made several trips to England, studying at Oxford University, where he took a degree in 1881. In that year he was elected a member of the Cape Colony Parliament, and in 1890 became prime minister. Rhodes dreamed of a block of British territory from the Cape to Cairo. He was largely responsible for bringing Bechuanaland under British rule in 1882 and four years later formed the British

South Africa Company, which occupied Mashonaland and Matabeleland. These became the colony of Rhodesia in 1895.

In 1896 Rhodes was blamed for a disastrous raid on the Transvaal led by his friend Dr. Jameson. Rhodes resigned as prime minister. But his prestige was restored a few years later when he was able to persuade rebellious African chiefs to lay down their arms.

Rhodes left a fortune to establish scholarships to Oxford University for students of the British Empire, Germany, and the United States.

Rhodesia is a landlocked country situated in southern Africa. Most of the land is a plateau rising to 5,000 feet above sea level. As a result, most of Rhodesia does not have a tropical climate, although it lies in the tropics, but is pleasantly warm throughout the year.

Most Rhodesians are African Negroes. But about one-twentieth of the people are of European descent. Most Africans are farmers, but some work in the cities. Some go to South Africa or Zambia to become miners. Nearly a half of the land in Rhodesia can only be owned by Europeans. Many Europeans own large farms.

Farming is Rhodesia's main industry and tobacco is the chief export crop. Other important products include asbestos, chrome ore, maize and meat. The Kariba Dam on the Zambezi River provides electricity for Rhodesia's expanding industries.

In 1923, Rhodesia (then called Southern Rhodesia) became a self-governing British colony. This meant that it had its own government which handled internal affairs, but Britain retained real control.

In the 1960's, the European-dominated Rhodesian government demanded independence from Britain. But Britain refused and finally Rhodesia declared itself independent in November 1965. Britain declared this an illegal act and many countries, including Britain, restricted trade with Rhodesia. But this action failed

Above: Rhodesia's capital, Salisbury, is a spacious well-planned modern city.

Left: Location map of Rhodesia (black).

Below: Wildlife is protected in Rhodesia's many national parks. The giraffe is only one of her many native animals.

1119

to force Rhodesia to resume its former status as a British colony. In 1970, Rhodesia declared itself a republic and ceased to look upon the British Queen as the head of state. The British government made efforts to bring about a settlement with Rhodesia in 1972 but this failed because the Africans refused to accept any agreement that did not give them majority rule. In 1973, terrorists operating from Zambia made attacks on European people and property.

Facts and Figures
Area: 150,333 square miles.
Population: 5,400,000.
Capital: Salisbury.

Rhône is an important river of western Europe. From its source in the Swiss Alps, it flows westwards into Lake Geneva, then into France, where it turns southwards for the rest of its 405-mile course, finally entering the Mediterranean Sea by two mouths. The river's chief tributary, the Saône, joins it at Lyons. Ships on the Rhône reach the port of Marseilles by means of a canal. The Rhône provides hydro-electric power, and its valley is a rich wine, fruit, olives and silk producing area.

Rice is one of the most important crops in the world. It gives a higher production of food per acre than almost any other crop and can be grown year after year in the same fields without a decline in yield. About half of the world's people, living mostly in Asia, depend on rice for their main food. Rice is a cereal crop like wheat and maize, but it grows in warmer and wetter places than most other cereals. Most rice is grown in flooded fields called *paddy fields*. The rice grains that are eaten are the seeds of the rice plant.

The world's leading rice-growing countries are China and India which together account for over half of the total world production. Japan, Pakistan and Indonesia are next in importance. Rice is also grown in America and Australia, and in Europe, where Italy is the leading producer.

Farmers may grow rice by planting seeds in the fields directly, either by drilling holes for the seeds or scattering the seeds and ploughing them in. But many farmers raise young rice plants in carefully tended nursery beds. When the seedlings are about a month old, the farmers transplant them into the fields.

Some varieties of 'upland' rice survive on rain water alone, but many are grown

Left: The flooded rice fields are cleared of weeds by ploughs drawn by water-buffaloes. Below: The task of planting the seedlings and weeding the fields by hand falls mainly to women.

in paddy fields. As the rice grows, the fields are flooded with water that is allowed gradually to increase in depth. When the plants begin to ripen, the fields are drained. By this time the plants are between two and six feet tall. They are harvested, usually by hand, and threshed to remove the grain. In some countries, particularly the U.S.A., combine harvesters are now being used.

For eating, the outer shells of the grains are usually removed by a milling process. Rice is generally eaten boiled, and the grains soak up water and swell as they cook. Alcoholic drinks can also be made from rice, such as the Japanese rice 'wine' called *sake*. The outer shells can be used to make livestock feed and starch, and rice grains can be ground into flour.

Richard was the name of three kings of England who reigned between 1189 and 1485.

Richard III was last of the Yorkist kings. He is thought to have been a hunchback.

Richard I (1157-1199), was the third son of Henry II. He was called *Coeur de Lion* ('Lionheart') because of his personal courage and a legend that described his fighting a lion and tearing its heart out. There were many such legends about Richard (himself a poet) that were sung and told after his death. Richard rebelled twice unsuccessfully against his father before inheriting the throne in 1189. During his 10-year reign, he spent a total of only 5 months in England, a country that interested him little except as a convenient source of money with which to finance his wars on the continent of Europe and in the Holy Land.

In 1191 and 1192 he led a determined campaign against Saladin, in the Third Crusade, but failed to capture Jerusalem. On his return, he was captured in Vienna and held to ransom for a huge sum by King Henry VI of Germany. He was not released until 1194. Five years later, he was killed while attacking a French castle.

Richard II (1367-1400), younger son of Edward the Black Prince, came to the throne of England in 1377, on the death of his grandfather, Edward III. His uncle, John of Gaunt, Duke of Lancaster, ruled for him until he came of age.

Richard showed coolness and courage in quelling and dispersing the 100,000-strong Peasants' Revolt in 1381. He had many favourites and this made him enemies. In 1388, the barons executed many of these favourites. Richard had his revenge on the barons in 1397, when he had many of them imprisoned, exiled or executed. A year later he also banished a former supporter, Henry of Bolingbroke, the son of John of Gaunt. But in 1399 Bolingbroke returned, captured popular support and had Richard deposed. Richard was imprisoned in Pontefract Castle, and died a year later under mysterious circumstances.

Richard III (1452-1485), the last of the Plantagenets, was King of England from 1483. The third son of Richard, Duke of York, he loyally supported his brother Edward IV. When Edward died, Richard became guardian of his 12-year-old nephew, Edward V. The boy's mother tried to seize power, so Richard forestalled her by taking the throne for himself. He claimed that Edward and his young brother were illegitimate, and had them imprisoned in the Tower of London. They were never seen again.

Rumours about the fate of the young princes swung popular opinion against Richard. Henry Tudor, of the House of Lancaster, returned to England from exile. He met and killed Richard in a battle at Bosworth in 1485. This battle ended the Wars of the Roses and established the victor as King Henry VII.

Richelieu, Armand Jean du Plessis, Duc de (1585-1642), a French cardinal and statesman, was chief minister of France during the reign of Louis XIII. Richelieu became bishop of Lucon in 1606, and with the friendship of the Queen Mother, consolidated his influence over the king. He became a cardinal in 1622 and Louis's chief minister two years later. From that time on, his ambition was to ensure the absolute power of the monarchy and the increase of French influence abroad.

At home, he suppressed the nobles, and quashed the political power of the *Huguenots* (French Protestants) while still allowing them religious freedom. Abroad, he sided against the Habsburgs, and in 1635 took his country into the Thirty Years War.

Riding A Mesopotamian statuette dated *c.* 2000 B.C. provides the earliest evidence of horse-riding. Horse racing, sometimes called the national sport of England, has been popular since the 12th century. The earliest show-jumping took place in Paris in 1886. Equestrian events have been part of the Olympic Games since 1912, and include dressage (obedience tests).

Polo is a game for two mounted teams of four players each. The object is to strike a ball with a long-handled mallet into a goal 8 yards wide and 10 feet high. Its origins go back to ancient Persia, but it was introduced to England in 1869 from India, a code of rules being issued by the Hurlingham Club in 1874.

Horse racing takes three main forms: flat racing; steeplechasing (in which a number of fences and ditches are introduced as obstacles), and point-to-point, a cross-country obstacle race from one point to another.

Chester, the oldest racecourse, was opened in 1540. The English 'classics' are the 1,000 Guineas, 2,000 Guineas, Derby, Oaks and St. Leger. The most famous steeplechase is the Grand National, first run in 1839.

The oldest stakes race in America is the Phoenix Handicap, started in 1831. America's 'Triple Crown' comprises the Kentucky Derby, Preakness Stakes and Belmont Stakes.

Steeplechasing and flat racing are popular all over the world. In Australia, the Melbourne Cup was first run in 1861 and remains one of the most important races today.

Above: Some of the world's finest horsemanship can be seen in the magnificent displays at the Spanish Riding School in Vienna.
Left: The hunt is a colourful, yet controversial part of the English country scene.

The popular sport of show-jumping calls for skill and co-operation of horse and rider.

Show jumping competitions are held indoors or outdoors in arenas of varying size, obstacles being so placed about the arena to test horses' ability to jump both height and distance.

Obstacles include walls, gates, hedges, fences and water jumps. Competitors are penalized for faults, the winner being the horse and rider with least penalty points. Competitions are also held against the clock, and to test high-jumping ability, the height of obstacles being increased with each succeeding round.

The official high jump record in 1969 was 8 ft. 1¼ ins. set by Huaso, ridden by Capt. A. L. Morales (Chile) at Santiago, Chile, on February 5, 1949, though unofficially a height of 9 ft. 6 ins. has been claimed. The long jump record over water is 27 ft. 2¾ ins. by Amada Mio ridden by Col. Lopez del Hierro (Spain) at Barcelona, Spain, on November 12, 1951.

Rio de Janeiro (pop. 4,297,000) is a city and seaport of Brazil. It lies on a narrow strip of land between mountains and sea on the western side of the Bay of Guanabara. For more than a hundred years before April 1960, on the inauguration of the new Brasília, it was the country's capital. It remains one of the chief commercial centres of South America. It is also the main port of Brazil. Brazil is a great coffee-producing country supplying the major portion of the world's need, and much of it passes through the port.

The Avenida Rio Branco, running from the docks in the north to Botafogo Bay in the south, is lined with elegant public buildings. The National Library, the National Museum, and the National Museum of Fine Art are excellent modern structures. Cultural institutions include academies for art and science.

1123

Left: The sheer walls of the Santa Elena canyon, rising 1,500 feet above the Rio Grande, show the power of a fast-flowing river to erode the land. Right: A waterfall is a temporary irregularity in a river's course which will be eventually worn away. Above: In 'old age' a river winds sluggishly in great loops across a plain and has little power to wear away the land.

Rivers Most rivers begin, unspectacularly, as a trickling stream of water from a melting glacier or from a tiny spring high in the hills or mountains. This stream is joined by others as it flows through the mountains and along the plains towards the sea. These side branches of the river are called its *tributaries.*

The area which is drained by the river and its tributaries is known as the *river basin.* The largest river basin in the world is that of the Amazon in South America, which drains almost three million square miles. The main river itself is 3,900 miles long, only 250 miles shorter than the Nile, the world's longest river.

Naturally enough, rivers rise on each side of a mountain range and form separate river systems. The line of separation between the two systems is called a *divide,* or *watershed.* The Great Divide in North America, for example, runs along the Rocky Mountains. It separates the rivers flowing westwards towards the

Pacific Ocean from those flowing eastwards towards the Atlantic Ocean.

Rivers, whether they are in Brazil or Britain, develop in much the same way. Three fairly distinct stages of development can be recognized which are often appropriately termed youth, maturity, and old age. In *youth,* up in the mountains, the river is unpredictable and full of vigour. In *maturity,* it runs at a more leisurely pace through well-formed valleys. In *old age*, it weaves rather aimlessly over a wide, level, featureless plain.

In the mountains, the river is narrow, but swift-flowing down steep slopes. The running water carries along with it pieces of rock that cut into and deepen the stream bed. The swirling, stone-filled waters drill pot-holes that eventually merge to lower the bed. The river valley

Opposite: Falls on the Nile, the world's longest river. The Ancient Egyptian civilization grew up on its flood plain.

Top: Rivers provide a means of communication and transportation. Most great cities have grown from settlements along river banks. Above: In the past many people lived in huts built on stilts in rivers for protection. Some still do in eastern lands. Right: In lands with a marked dry season many rivers dry up for part of the year.

at this stage is deep, narrow, and steep-sided.

Where parts of the bed are softer than others, they will be worn away more quickly, and rapids and waterfalls will form. (See Waterfalls.) Very deep and extensive rapids are called *cataracts*.

The river valley gradually widens out as tributaries join the main stream. The gradient, or slope, of the river becomes more gentle. Large amounts of

transported material settle out as the river slows down. Gradually the river begins to *meander*, or swing from side to side of the valley. This serves to widen the valley. In times of flood, the river covers the whole of the valley floor. It washes down and deposits sand, gravel, and rocks to form a so-called *flood plain*. The steep sides of the valley which mark the limit of the flood plain are called *bluffs*.

As the land becomes flatter, the river slows down, and more and more material is deposited. The meanders become more pronounced because the current attacks the outside of the bends more than the inside. Material is deposited in the quiet waters on the inside of the bends. At this stage *oxbow lakes* can occur. When a river meanders in a loop, the river can erode away the 'neck' of the loop until the two ends join up and the river runs straight. The ends of the loop will then become silted up and a horse-shoe shaped lake will be formed.

In old age, then, the river has cut its way down practically to sea-level and has a vast flood plain extending back from the sea. Sometimes the sea-level drops or the land rises. This increases the speed of the river, and it begins cutting a new valley for itself through the old flood plain. This process is called *rejuvenation*, because the river once more has the vigour of its youth. When this process happens several times, a series of *river terraces* are formed. They are notable features of most river valleys.

When the river enters the sea, it slows down and deposits the fine sand and mud it is carrying. Usually the action of the sea tends to push the deposits back up river, and constantly shifting sand-bars are formed.

But in a tideless sea, such as the Mediterranean, there is nothing to check the outflow and deposition of material by the river. This material gradually builds up and extends seawards in a roughly triangular shape to form a *delta*. As the delta builds up, the river gradually splits up into a number of channels, or *distributaries*. The best-known examples of deltas are those of the Nile, Ganges, and Mississippi. (See Delta.)

The world's longest river is the Nile. It is 4,160 miles long. The Amazon in South America is the second longest at 3,900 miles, but it carries more water than the Nile. It discharges on average over 4 million cubic feet of water per second into the Atlantic Ocean.

Road transport Until the end of the 1800's road transport was either on horse back or in a wheeled vehicle drawn by horses or other animals such as oxen. Many different styles of vehicle evolved throughout the ages—from the Roman two-wheeled chariot to the four-wheeled stage coach of the Wild West.

In 1784 a system of horse-drawn fast mail coaches was established in Britain with fresh teams of horses kept at inns along the roads and by the 1820's fast passenger-carrying stage-coaches served most of the country's main roads. But from 1840 on-wards the rapid growth of railways brought an end to the stage-coach era. Unable to compete with the railways on long-distance journeys, road transport was reduced to local carts in the country and horse-cabs or buses in towns.

At the end of the nineteenth century new forms of road transport appeared. The electric tram was developed in Germany and came to Britain in the 1880's. Gottlieb Daimler built his first automobile in 1886, though automobiles did not appear in Britain until 1894. At first motoring was a rich man's hobby, but by 1914 petrol-driven buses and lorries (trucks) were being used. In 1910, Henry Ford began to sell the first cheap automobile, his Model T, in the U.S.A.

Since 1918 trucks have become bigger and faster and carry more and more goods. Buses and coaches have replaced many railway services and everywhere fast, cheap automobiles crowd the roads, used by people of all classes for business and pleasure. New multi-lane highways have had to be built for this traffic, but in many large cities traffic congestion is still a major problem.

Above: In some countries primitive ox-drawn carts are still a common sight.
Above right: In the early 1800's carriages were owned by most wealthy families. The barouche was especially popular. In it the ladies could take the air and greet their friends during leisurely drives.
Right: A system of fast horse-drawn mail coaches, with fresh teams of horses stationed at inns along the roads was established in 1784.

Right: A model of the 'B' Type omnibus. This was the first standard type bus introduced by the London General Omnibus Company in 1910.

Another drawback of the automobile is pollution caused by exhaust fumes. Some countries are passing laws to control the amounts of gases emitted.

Roads Every country in the world is building new roads and reconstructing old ones in order to cope with the ever-increasing volume of motor traffic. Already there are well over 100 million automobiles using the world's roads.

In some continents, such as Africa, many roads are little more than flattened dirt tracks which turn 'into mud after heavy rain and to choking dust clouds in the dry season.

Europe has a very extensive network of roads. A large number are narrow and

As more and more people buy private cars existing road networks become increasingly crowded.

twisty and not really suitable for high-speed motor traffic. Most roads in the United States, on the other hand, are straight. But American road builders had a distinct advantage over European builders. They had plenty of space and were not tied to ancient road systems.

Most countries now, however, have networks of wide, straight roads built especially for motor vehicles. In Britain, this kind of road is called a *motorway*; in France, *autoroute*; in Italy, *autostrada*; in Germany, *autobahn* and in the United States, *superhighway*.

These high-speed roads are designed so that traffic going in opposite directions is clearly separated. They are made with gentle curves and easy gradients so that vehicles do not have to slow down. There are no junctions on these roads. Other roads pass over them at flyovers or under them at underpasses.

The building of strong, straight roads is not, however, a modern development. The Ancient Romans built such roads 2,000 years ago. They laid a bed of large stone blocks, covered with small broken stones and sand, with more blocks on top.

After the Romans, there were no notable road builders in Europe until the 1700's and 1800's. Thomas Telford, a brilliant canal and bridge builder, also

Above: Multi-lane highways are needed to cope with the ever-increasing volume of road traffic. Today, there are well over 100 million automobiles in the world, many of them concentrated in the densely populated parts of Europe and North America.
The use of machines has greatly increased the speed of road building.
Right: A fine-grading machine gives an even surface to the subgrade on which the road is built.
Top right: Laying a concrete top surface or pavement. Machines spread the concrete evenly over the base and compact it.
Below: Motorways are designed to ensure a smooth flow of traffic. Flyovers and underpasses carry vehicles from one road to another at different levels without interrupting the streams of traffic.

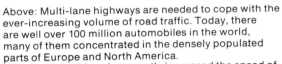

built 1,000 miles of roads. He used large stones as a foundation, covered with broken stones, and then gravel.

The greatest road builder of them all, John Loudon McAdam, used several layers of broken stone instead of large ones as foundations. Modern road builders use similar kinds of foundations.

The first stage in building a modern highway is to survey the countryside to find the best route to take. This route will avoid as many obstacles as possible in order to keep expensive operations such as bridge building to a minimum.

Preparation of the chosen route begins with levelling and firming the ground. This is done by earth-moving machines, such as bulldozers, scrapers, and excavators. On top of this levelled ground, or *subgrade,* is laid a *base* and often a *sub-base* of crushed stone.

The top surface, or *pavement,* is laid on top of the base. A rigid pavement is made of concrete. Machines spread the concrete evenly over the base and compact it. A flexible pavement consists of small broken stones held together by tar. This mixture is called tarmacadam, or tarmac. Asphalt is a similar material. It is spread hot by machines and made firm by heavy rollers.

Talking points
* Today, increasing amounts of farming land and housing are being destroyed to provide space for new roads for the fast growing number of cars. Would it be fair to say that the car has become more important than people?
* Why are many roads in countries like Britain narrow and twisting while in other countries such as the United States they tend to run in straight lines?
* What effect would the building of a new road across the countryside have on the wildlife that lives in the area? Can you think of any animal or bird that would benefit from it?
Articles to read
Automobile; Motor cycle; Motor sport; Pollution; Road transport.

Rockets At first there appears to be little in common between the small firework rocket and the 360-foot-high vehicle which takes astronauts to the Moon. But both rockets work on the same principle. They burn fuel to produce hot gases which shoot out backwards to push the rocket forwards. It is not the escaping gases *themselves* which provide the forward

thrust, but the reaction produced by the mass of hot gases being thrown backwards from the rocket.

Rockets can operate in the vacuum of space because they carry their own oxygen as well as fuel, unlike the jet engines of aircraft which use the oxygen in the atmosphere. The substance that provides oxygen to burn the rocket fuel is called an *oxidant.* Both fuel and oxidant are called *propellents.* They can be either liquid or solid.

Left: Burning fuel in a rocket engine produces hot gases which by escaping rearwards move the rocket forwards. This principle of reaction can be demonstrated with a balloon. When the neck is untied the balloon is driven forwards by the reaction produced by the gases being thrown out backwards.
Below: Nike-Hercules anti-aircraft missiles being tested in New Mexico, U.S.A.

Liquid propellents are usually the most powerful. They are used in the rockets which launch spacecraft. Liquid hydrogen and kerosene (paraffin) are widely used as rocket fuels. Liquid oxygen is the most widely used oxidant.

The engine of a liquid-propellent rocket is quite simple. Fuel and oxidant are pumped from storage tanks through control valves into an open-ended chamber where they are burnt. The propellents enter this combustion chamber as a fine mist so that they mix and burn easily. The hot gases produced leave the chamber through a nozzle at very high speed and thrust the rocket forwards.

Solid-propellent rockets are even simpler. They consist of a combustion chamber filled with propellent and a nozzle. Firework rockets have a solid propellent, such as gunpowder. Guided missiles and the retro-rockets of spacecraft have solid propellents, too.

Most of the bulk of a space rocket is taken up with propellents to provide the power to lift spacecraft off the ground against the Earth's gravity. But a single rocket cannot by itself lift a heavy load into orbit. Several rockets must be joined together, one on top of the other, to provide the necessary power.

Rockets built in this way are called *multi-stage*, or *step* rockets. Most space vehicles have a massive first, booster-stage, and two smaller stages. Each stage fires in turn and thrusts the vehicle ever higher. The vehicle gets lighter and lighter as the spent stages separate.

The rocket is not a recent invention. The Chinese used rockets in warfare as long ago as the 1200's. But few significant developments took place until the 1900's. In 1903, Konstantin Tsiolkovsky in Russia published the first scientific paper on rocket propulsion. In 1923, the German Hermann Oberth published his famous book *Rocket into Interplanetary Space*. Three years later, Robert Hutchings Goddard in the United States fired the first liquid-propellent rocket.

Above: Rockets can operate in the vacuum of space because they carry their own oxygen as well as fuel. The substance that provides oxygen to burn the rocket fuel is called an oxidant. Both fuel and oxidant are called propellents. They can be either liquid or solid. Liquid propellents are usually the more powerful. Kerosene (paraffin) is normally used for the fuel, and liquid oxygen for the oxidant. Fuel and oxidant are pumped from storage tanks into an open-ended chamber where they are burnt. Solid propellents are used in guided missiles, fireworks and most retro-rockets.

Below: A liquid propellent multi-stage rocket stands ready for launching.

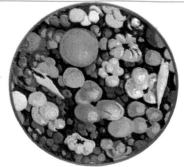

Globigerina Ooze

Mixed Ooze of Mollusc and Pteropod Shells

Above: The ocean floors are covered by various oozes, formed from the skeletons of marine organisms. These will eventually be turned into solid rock by pressure or by cementation.

Above: Conglomerate is formed of individual pebbles cemented together by silica or lime.
Below: The layered arrangement of sedimentary rocks can often be seen in cliff and quarry sections.

By 1942 the Germans had developed the V-2 rocket which Hitler later used to bombard London. After the war, both the Americans and the Russians developed multi-stage rockets, which they realised could carry satellites into orbit. And in 1957 Russia sent up the first satellite, *Sputnik 1*.

Rocks form the material that makes up the Earth's crust. Most rocks are hidden from view by grass, trees and other plants. Plants grow in the thin layer of soil which covers most rocks. (See Soil.) Exposed rock appears in such places as cliffs and desert areas, where there are few plants and no soil. Scientists divide rocks into three main types: *igneous, sedimentary* and *metamorphic*.

Deep under the Earth are pockets of hot molten rock called *magma*. When a volcano erupts, magma often flows from it as streams of *lava*. Sometimes the magma solidifies underground. Any rock formed from solidified magma is an *igneous* rock. Igneous rocks include basalt, granite and pumice. The word 'igneous' comes from the Latin word 'ignis' meaning 'fire'.

Throughout the history of the Earth, rivers and other natural forces have been *eroding* (wearing away) the land. Weather conditions cause rocks to decay and crumble. Rivers sweep rock fragments towards the sea or into lakes. There the fragments of sand, gravel and mud pile up in beds as *sediments*. These sediments are

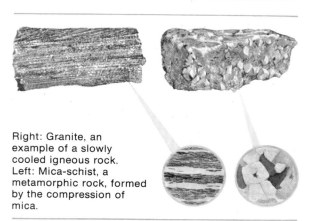

Right: Granite, an example of a slowly cooled igneous rock.
Left: Mica-schist, a metamorphic rock, formed by the compression of mica.

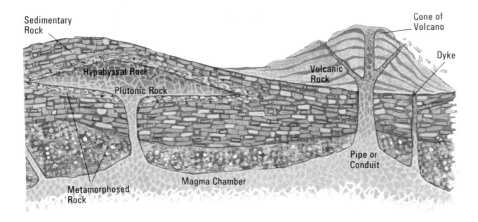

Sedimentary Rock
Hypabyssal Rock
Plutonic Rock
Metamorphosed Rock
Magma Chamber
Volcanic Rock
Cone of Volcano
Dyke
Pipe or Conduit

Left: Igneous rocks are those that have cooled from molten material. Lava ejected during a volcanic eruption and cooling quickly on the surface of the Earth forms fine-grained volcanic rocks such as basalt. Molten matter cooling slowly beneath the Earth's surface forms coarse-grained plutonic rocks such as granite.

eventually pressed into solid rock called *sedimentary* rock. Rocks formed in this way include sandstones, formed from grains of sand, and shales, formed from clay. Sedimentary rocks often contain the remains of creatures that once lived in the water. Buried in the sediments, these remnants are sometimes squeezed into solid rock to form *fossils*. (See Fossils.) Some sedimentary rocks are composed almost entirely of the remains of living things. For example, coal was formed from plants. Many limestones were formed from the remains of sea creatures.

Some sedimentary rocks were formed from minerals that were once dissolved in water. When the water evaporated, the minerals crystallized to form such rocks as rock salt and phosphate rocks.

Metamorphic rocks are rocks whose appearance and sometimes chemical composition have been changed by terrific heat or great pressure. Sometimes the action of steam and gas also changes rocks. For example, great pressure has turned shale, a sedimentary rock, into hard slate. Limestone has been changed into marble.

The study of rocks is part of *geology*.

Geology is important because rocks have many uses. Some rocks are used for building houses and roads. Some contain ores of valuable metals or minerals, or radioactive elements such as radium and uranium. Geologists can also locate some layers of rock which contain great reservoirs of petroleum and natural gas.

Geologists have also discovered much about the history of the Earth from studying rocks. They have traced the development of living things from the study of fossils. They have proved that sedimentary rocks containing fossils were formed in ancient seas millions of years ago. Great pressures from within the Earth often squeezed up these rocks into high mountain chains. Even the rocks of Mount Everest, the world's highest mountain, were once sediments under the sea. (See Mountains.)

Rocky Mountains The Rockies, as they are usually called, form the main mountain system of North America. The Rockies run down the western side of North America for more than 2,200 miles, from Alaska to New Mexico. In some places they

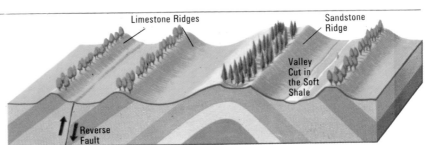

Tremendous forces in the Earth's crust have bent twisted and fractured the layers of rock in many places. Bends in the rock are called folds; fractures are called faults.

Limestone Ridges
Sandstone Ridge
Valley Cut in the Soft Shale
Reverse Fault

are 350 miles wide. They are part of the enormous Cordilleran chain that extends from the Arctic Circle to Cape Horn. In North America the Cordillera is 4,000 miles long and 1,000 miles wide at its greatest extent. The highest peak is Mount McKinley (20,320 ft). In Mexico the chain is called *Sierra Madre*, and from Panama southwards through South America it is known as the *Andes*.

The main peaks of the Rockies are Mt Logan (19,850 ft) in the Yukon and North West Territories; Mt Robson (12,972 ft) in British Columbia; Mt Elbert (14,431 ft) in Colorado; and Fremont's Peak (13,781 ft) in Wyoming. In the Canadian Rockies there are several mountains that are more than 12,000 feet high. In Colorado there are 55 peaks that exceed 14,000 ft, and 10 peaks in New Mexico and Utah rise to more than 13,000 feet.

The Rockies are famed for their wild and beautiful scenery. They present a picture of jagged, snow-capped peaks and torrential rivers dashing through rocky gorges. Some of the greatest rivers in the continent rise in the Rockies. These include the Missouri, the Colorado, the Rio Grande, the Columbia and the Arkansas.

The lower slopes of the Rockies are covered in grassland and are used for cattle ranching. Further up the mountains, forests of fir and spruce eventually peter out into scrub and thin grassy patches. Some crops are grown in the fertile areas in the summer. These include wheat, barley and potatoes. The mountains also abound in wildlife. Grizzly bears, pumas, big-horn sheep, and deer are frequently hunted.

The Rockies are millions of years old and still show some signs of volcanic activity, as in the boiling natural geysers of Yellowstone National Park.

Rodents form the largest *order* (major group) of mammals, consisting of nearly 2,000 *species* (distinct kinds). They all have large, curved *incisors* (front teeth) that are specially developed for gnawing. They are curved, and grow continuously; as the animal gnaws they wear down. Their front surface consists of hard enamel, which wears away more slowly than the rest. This results in the sharp, chisel-like edge.

There are three main groups of rodents: the squirrel group, which also includes beavers, marmots and gophers; the mouse

Right: A Rocky mountain bighorn sheep stands beside the Trail Ridge road in the Rocky Mountain National Park.

Below: Against a background of snow-capped peaks, torrential streams and rivers carve their way through forests of fir and spruce.

Opposite: The grey squirrel is a rodent. His large bushy tail helps him balance as he jumps from tree to tree.

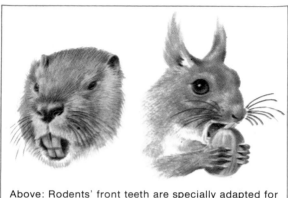

Above: Rodents' front teeth are specially adapted for gnawing. The rate at which the chisel-like teeth wear away is roughly matched by the rate of their continuous growth.

Below: There are nearly 2,000 different kinds of rodents. These are some of the ground-living ones.
1. Prairie dog
2. Chipmunk
3. Ground squirrel
4. American woodchuck
5. Rat.

group, which includes rats, hamsters, lemmings and voles; and the porcupine group. Most rodents are only a few inches long, but the biggest, the capybara of South America, may reach a length of four feet.

Rodeo is a popular form of entertainment in the western parts of the United States and Canada. At a rodeo, spectators can enjoy watching a variety of cowboy skills. They include contests among amateurs and exhibitions by professionals who travel round from show to show. People at a rodeo wear traditional western out-fits — high boots, blue jeans, and wide-brimmed hats.

Many rodeo events involve a test of riding skill, such as *bronco riding*. A bronco is an untamed horse. It bucks and lurches in an attempt to throw its rider. In *bareback riding* contests, a cowboy has no saddle and no reins to hold. He tries to stay on his mount for at least 10 seconds. In *saddle bronc riding*, the rider has a saddle and reins. But he is allowed to hold on only with one hand. In other events, cowboys compete in riding bulls.

Rodeos also include an event in which cowboys compete in roping a calf. The winner of this contest is the one who can bring the calf down and tie three of its feet in the shortest time. In the *bull-dogging* event, a cowboy wrestles a bull to the ground by its horns. Many rodeos also feature performances of lassoing skill and shooting skill.

Today the rodeo is mainly a show put on for fun. But it was once a contest of skill among real working cowboys. The rodeo took place at round-up — the gathering of the herds at the railhead.

Roman Empire Rome began as a village on the banks of the River Tiber. The traditional date of its foundation is 753 B.C., when it is supposed to have been founded by Romulus, who gave the new settlement his name. It was certainly inhabited some time soon after 1000

B.C. Rome gradually became the leader of the nearby towns, which were formed into the *Latin League*. In the sixth century foreigners, called Etruscans, conquered Rome and began to rule the town. They were expelled in 509 B.C. and Rome became a republic.

Republican Rome was ruled by two elected consuls or magistrates, chosen from the patricians or richer citizens. They were helped to govern by various assemblies. The most important assembly was the senate of which the head of every leading family was a member.

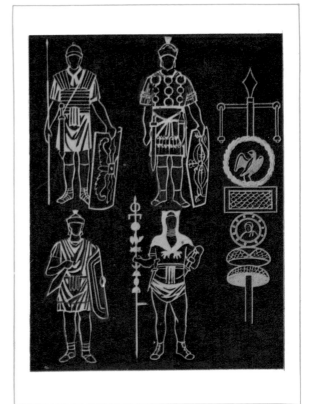

Right: Within the Roman army there were many different ranks and types of soldiers, including legionaries (top left), centurions (top right), auxiliaries (bottom left), and standard bearers (bottom right). The standard had a golden eagle at its top, with golden wreaths, medals and plaques underneath to commemorate battles in which the legion had fought well.
Below: The remains of the forum, the market place and meeting place, where the business of government and private citizens was carried on. This remarkable group of public buildings was once the very heart of the Roman Empire.

Above: Wherever the Romans went they built magnificent buildings. The remains of ancient arches, temples, amphitheatres, baths, and forums can still be seen in many places in Europe and North Africa.

The poorer citizens, the plebeians, struggled for centuries to gain equal rights. In 287 B.C. officials called *tribunes* were appointed to protect the interests of the lower classes.

Rome was one of the earliest states to have a detailed code of law. The Twelve Tables, Rome's first written laws, were set down in 451 and 450 B.C.

After 450 B.C. Rome began to expand. By 270 B.C. she had established her power throughout Italy, up to the northern ridge of the Apennines. The conquest of Sicily brought Rome into conflict with Carthage (see Carthage). Next Rome began to conquer other lands on the shores of the Mediterranean, and was soon ruling Spain, North Africa, Narbonese Gaul (southern France, Provence), Greece and part of Asia Minor. Rome also

controlled, though she did not rule directly, Syria, Egypt and many other states.

Rome was successful in conquering these states because of her excellent army. Her soldiers were brave, well trained and disciplined. The Romans built good roads through all the lands they conquered. In case of revolt, soldiers could march swiftly down these roads and reach the trouble spot. Colonies of Roman citizens were set up in the conquered states. They had special privileges and were allowed to share in the governing of the towns. These towns served as an advertisement for the Roman way of life. People who visited them admired the fine buildings, the public baths, the Forum (market place) and saw the benefits of Roman rule.

As the Roman empire expanded, her citizens grew richer. The old Roman way of life changed for the worse. The citizens began to rely on slaves to work for them, and treated them with great brutality. Roman farming was neglected, because cheaper corn could be imported from North Africa. A century of civil war followed as a struggle for power took place.

Julius Caesar was the victor in this struggle. By 45 B.C. he became dictator

Below: The map shows the spread of the Roman Empire from the beginning of the 1st Punic War (264 B.C.) to its greatest extent under Trajan A.D. 117.

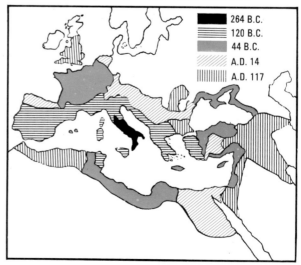

■	264 B.C.
≡	120 B.C.
▨	44 B.C.
▨	A.D. 14
‖‖‖	A.D. 117

of the Roman state for life. He was too cautious to call himself king; but his enemies feared his power and assassinated him. Caesar's nephew Octavian seized power after his uncle's death. He became the first Emperor of Rome, under the name of Augustus. Under his wise rule the Pax Romana, Roman peace, was maintained. Augustus decided to stop extending the frontiers of the Empire. Wars against the German tribes had not been successful and Augustus fixed the rivers Rhine and Danube as the northern limits of the Empire.

Towards the end of Augustus' reign Christianity grew up as a religion. Later emperors persecuted the Christians until, in A.D. 313, the Emperor Constantine announced that they were to be allowed freedom of worship. He also established the city of Byzantium (later Constantinople, today Istanbul) as the capital of the eastern half of the Empire. After A.D. 395 rule over the Empire was divided between two emperors, one in Rome and the other in Byzantium.

From the fifth century A.D. the Empire began to decline. Barbarian tribes had long been attacking her northern and eastern frontiers. Within the Empire there were many problems; people were discontented because of high taxes and the government officials were no longer efficient and honest. A huge slave population meant a constant fear of rebellion. Trade and agriculture had also declined.

Waves of invaders began to break through the Roman frontiers. Alaric, the chief of the Visigoths, sacked Rome in A.D. 410. Other invaders, Franks, Vandals and Huns swept into the Empire and ravaged it. Many of them settled down and intermarried with the people they had conquered, adopting many of their ways. Only the eastern half of the Empire remained free until the Turkish conquest of 1453. The western half split into many small kingdoms, which developed over the centuries into modern nations like Spain and France.

A view across Rome, looking down the piazza designed by Bernini from the roof of St. Peter's Basilica.

Rome (pop. 2,843,000) is the capital of Italy. It occupies both banks of the River Tiber, 17 miles from the mouth in the Tyrrhenian Sea. It is the largest city in the country, and an important manufacturing and trade centre.

Rome is a city of many beautiful churches and the great religious centre of the Roman Catholic Church. The Basilica of St. John Lateran is the cathedral church and the Episcopal seat of the Pontiff, Archbishop of Rome. The Vatican (an independent state), on the right bank of the river, is the seat and Apostolic Residence of the Pope. The Papal Palace, with its art collection and museum, and the great Basilica of St. Peter are particularly famous.

The city is a great cultural centre of Europe, with many universities and colleges of higher learning. The museums and art galleries, rich in art treasures, attract visitors from all over the world.

According to tradition the city was founded by Romulus in the year 753 B.C. with a small settlement on the Palatine Hill. In the course of time this combined with similar settlements on Capitoline, Aventine, Caelian, Esquiline, Quirinale

1139

and Viminale — the seven hills of Rome — and in the valleys between. It became the centre of Latin civilization and the capital of the great Roman Empire of the ancient world.

Rome is a shrine of ancient history and art. Its classical monuments — ruined forums, triumphal arches, amphitheatres, temples and baths — vividly recall the race whose brilliance so influenced civilization as it is known today.

Roosevelt, Franklin Delano (1882-1945), was president of the United States during the Second World War. He served for 12 years — longer than any other president. He inspired people by his leadership. He got the country on its feet again after the *depression* (failure of businesses) of 1929. In 1941 he brought the U.S.A. into the war. Roosevelt was the first leader to speak to millions of people on the radio to explain what he was doing.

Roosevelt was born at Hyde Park, in New York state. His Dutch ancestors had gone to the United States in 1649. He studied at Harvard and Columbia universities, and became a barrister in 1907. In 1921 he was crippled by polio, and spent most of the rest of his life in a wheelchair. But this only made him work harder. He became Governor of New York state in 1928, and president of the United States in 1933.

Left: With a characteristically friendly gesture Franklin Roosevelt returns the greetings of the people of Britain on a visit to London.

The changes that Roosevelt made because of the depression and poverty were called the New Deal. The government organized various kinds of work, such as building dams and farming. In this way he gave work to millions of starving men. He also set up schemes for sickness benefits and pensions.

Roosevelt gave much aid and support to Britain in the Second World War before the United States entered the conflict. The 'Big Three' meetings of Roosevelt, Churchill, and Stalin became famous. As the war drew to a close Roosevelt's health began to fail, and he died before the final defeat of Germany and Japan.

Root crops are the crops we grow for their roots or tubers (swollen underground stems). They include many vegetables, and a few sweet plants. Root crops are good to eat as they contain large amounts of starch, an energy-giving substance.

The commonest root vegetable in temperate countries is the potato. This plant grew originally in South America, but is now cultivated all over the world (see Potatoes). In the tropics, the most important vegetable is the yam, whose tubers grow to a large size. Other root vegetables of warm regions include the cocoyam of Africa, the cassava of South America and the sweet potato. Other temperate root vegetables include swedes, turnips, mangels, carrots, parsnips, radishes and beetroot.

The most important sweet root crop is sugar beet. This crop is an important source of sugar in temperate regions (see Sugar). Other sweet root crops include arrowroot, used to make tapioca.

Roots are organs that anchor plants to the soil. They also absorb water and mineral salts from the soil to supply the plant's needs. There are two kinds of root systems. A *tap root* consists of one major root from which various minor

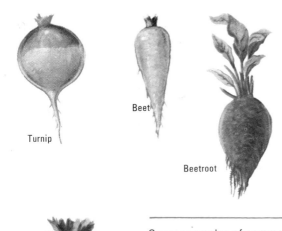

Turnip

Beet

Beetroot

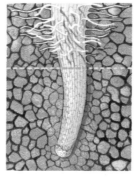

Left: An enlarged root-tip showing the cap and the region of growth (below the dotted line). The soil particles are compressed by growth pressure. Below: The tap-root system of the thistle and the fibrous system of a grass.

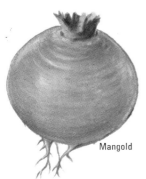

Mangold

Some examples of common root crops.

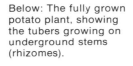

Below: The fully grown potato plant, showing the tubers growing on underground stems (rhizomes).

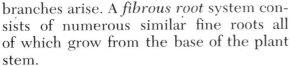

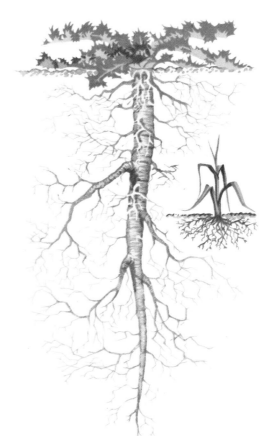

branches arise. A *fibrous root* system consists of numerous similar fine roots all of which grow from the base of the plant stem.

Roots grow at the tip. Cells in this region divide and enlarge, pushing the free end of the root through the soil. The delicate end of the root is protected from damage in the soil by a cap of cells over its tip. These root-cap cells get worn away as the root pushes through the soil, and are replaced by new cells all the

time. If you look just behind the tip of a root you will see an area covered with tiny thread-like outgrowths. These are root hairs, which absorb water and mineral salts from the soil.

Water is drawn into root cells by a process called *osmosis*. Water diffuses from a region where the concentration of water molecules is high—the water in the soil—to a place where it is not so high—the cell sap in the root. Water absorbed by the root hairs moves from cell to cell across the root until it enters the conducting tissue—the xylem cells. Conducting tissue is continuous from the tips of the roots right through the stem to the edges of every leaf. Hence, water absorbed from the soil can quickly get to any part of the plant.

Roots are also food-storage organs, where many perennial plants house food reserves for renewed growth in the following spring.

Rose family is a huge family of plants (Rosaceae), found in most parts of the world. In addition to the well known garden rose, there are some 2,000 *species* (kinds) belonging to this important family. They include trees, shrubs and herbs. Among them are fruit trees such as the apple, cherry, peach, pear, apricot and quince; shrubs such as raspberries, blackberries and roses; runners such as strawberries; and finally ornamental plants such as mountain ash, hawthorn and spiraea.

All members of the rose family are seed-bearing and *dicotyledonous*, which means that each sprout has two leaves. The flowers are often showy, and are arranged in a regular form—each with five petals and five *sepals* (green, leaf-like units that make up the outer ring of flower parts known as the *calyx*). The leaves grow *alternately* on the stem—that is, they are not placed opposite one another but appear one by one in a line twisting round the stem. The leaves vary widely in detail and texture, but most of the tropical members of the family (trees and shrubs) have leathery, evergreen leaves. The fruits of the rose family are often, but not always, fleshy.

There are six recognized sub-families in the group. The first consists mainly of shrubs bearing many small pink, purple, or white flowers. They are typified by spiraea. The second and largest, comprising more than 1,000 species, is characterized by its swollen or cup-shaped fruits, as the strawberry. The third sub-family

has large, fleshy fruits with a core at the centre holding the seeds. Apples, pears and quinces belong to this group. The fourth sub-family is made up of a group of small herbs found in dry regions of Africa and India. The fifth sub-family, to which the plum belongs, has a fruit made up of one seed with a hard cover, the 'stone'. The last sub-family includes a large number of tropical, evergreen trees and shrubs, mostly originating from South America.

Roses are handsome flowering shrubs or climbing plants popular with gardeners in almost all parts of the world. Cultivated roses grow in any reasonable soil, and some kinds bloom continuously through the growing season. Wild roses, from which all garden varieties derive, have simple blooms. A ring of five separate petals surrounds numerous stamens (male parts) and carpels (female parts). Cultivated forms have fewer stamens and more petals.

Gardeners class roses as bush, standard, and climbing roses. *Bush roses* have a main stem that branches just above soil level; *standard roses* bloom on branches that arise at the top of a single stem three or four feet high; *climbing roses* grow several feet high on highly branched, vigorous shoots.

Perhaps one of the most popular and the most widespread groups of bush roses are the *hybrid teas*. These were derived by crossing hybrid perpetual roses with tea roses. Hybrid teas combine the large, colourful flowers of the perpetuals with the long flowering season of the teas.

In the Northern Hemisphere roses are best planted in November. The soil must be well-prepared and all roots of perennial weeds should be dug out. Newly planted roses need to be pruned back hard, reducing shoots to ease the burden of recovering roots. Pruning techniques for established roses differ from variety to variety.

Successful rose varieties are increased

The pear tree (right) and the strawberry (below) are both members of the rose family. The fruits of this family vary enormously in appearance, but one way of telling the members' relationship is by the five-petalled flowers.

Left: The briar rose is a simple, wild flower.

Right: Cultivated roses are often named after famous people. These two hybrid varieties are President Herbert Hoover hybrid tea (right) and Mrs John Laing hybrid perpetual (left).

Below: The China roses form a class of their own. They have tiny but perfect flowers.

by transferring buds from the cultivated forms on to the stems of vigorous and hardy wild varieties such as those of the dog rose. This process is known as *budding*.

Ross and Cromarty (area 3,090 square miles), a Highland county of Scotland, also includes Lewis and several smaller islands of the Outer Hebrides. Its county town is Dingwall, and its population is 58,000.

The county is ruggedly beautiful and mountainous, with some peaks exceeding 3,800 feet. The coastline is deeply indented and numerous sea *lochs* (lakes) run inland. Much of the county is covered with deer forests. Among the tourist attractions is the Glomach Falls, which at 370 feet is the highest in Britain. Sheep and cattle rearing is the main occupation. What cultivated land there is, is given over to oats and potatoes. Whisky is distilled and is almost the only industry. Stornoway is the largest town.

In 1749 Rousseau entered a competition in which entrants had to write about the effects of progress in the arts and sciences on morals. His entry won first prize and helped to bring him fame.

Rousseau, Jean-Jacques (1712-1778), was a French writer and philosopher, whose works greatly influenced the writers and thinkers of his time. We can discover much about him from his masterpiece *Confessions*, the autobiography which was not published till after his death.

Rousseau was born at Geneva, in Switzerland. His mother died soon after his birth and he was brought up by his father, a watchmaker. He was apprenticed to an engraver, but when he was 16 he ran away to Savoy, where he was helped and protected by Madame de Warens, a wealthy widow. He showed signs very early of an unstable personality, and led a wandering life for some years.

In 1742 he went to Paris and devised a new system of writing music, which attracted the notice of several influential people. His first important written works, *Discourse on the Influence of Learning and Art* (1750) and *Discourse on the Origin of Inequality* (1754), expressed his revolt against the existing social order.

La Nouvelle Heloise, a novel in letter form, appeared in 1761. The next year *Du Contrat Social* was published, in which Rousseau discusses his political philo-

The start of a canoeing race in the 1972 Olympics. The canoes are of the Kayak type.

sophy, which had great influence on French thought. He states that people should freely choose their own rulers.

In the same year, in *Emile,* he expounded his views on education, saying that children should be taught through an appeal to their curiosity and encouraged to express their own ideas. The book made Rousseau very unpopular, especially with the Roman Catholic Church, and he went into exile, first in Geneva then in England, until 1767. He spent his last years in Paris.

Rowing Races are normally held for eight-oared, four-oared or two-oared boats (known as 'pairs'), and for double-scullers and single-scullers. The eights also carry a coxswain, to steer them. Fours and pairs are sometimes rowed without a coxswain. In rowing, each member of the crew uses either one oar or two sculls, one in each hand.

The oldest sculling race is the Doggett's Coat and Badge, which began

August 1, 1716 and is still rowed annually on the river Thames over the 5 miles from London Bridge to Chelsea. The world professional sculling championship started in 1831.

The Oxford *v.* Cambridge Boat Race for 8-oared crews on the River Thames started in 1829. Up to 1973 Cambridge had won 67 times to Oxford's 51. A dead-heat was recorded in 1877. Yale and Harvard have their own annual Boat Race on the Thames, New London, Connecticut. The annual Henley Royal Regatta attracts a distinguished international entry.

Canoeing is the sport of propelling a light boat, by means of a paddle. In the 1972 Olympics there were races for single canoeists, pairs and fours in the Kayak and Canadian classes. The kayak is a decked canoe with one or more cockpits; the Canadian is open with a single-blade paddle, or paddles.

1145

Kayaks are used for races on rough waters through obstacles, known as slalom races.

Roxburgh (area 665 square miles) is a border county in the Southern Uplands of Scotland. Its county town is Jedburgh, and its population is 42,000.

The land is generally hilly, with the Cheviots spilling over the southern border from England. It is drained by the Teviot and the Tweed. Sheep breeding is the main occupation. The largest and most

Left: Tapping: latex oozes from a sloping cut in the tree into a collecting cup.
Below: Acid is added to the latex and then poured into separate coagulating pans.
Bottom: The sheets are cleaned and inspected for impurities.

important town is Hawick, where hosiery, woollen goods and knitwear are manufactured. Other towns are Kelso and Newtown St. Boswells, the administrative centre. The county is rich in monastic remains, particularly at Melrose.

Rubber is the flexible material from which tyres are made. It is an elastic material, but it is also airtight, waterproof, strong and long-wearing. These qualities make rubber the only material that can be used for tyres. But rubber has many other uses. Rubber bands hold things together. Many balls are made of or contain rubber. Hoses and belts are made of rubber for use in industry. And we use rubbers to erase pencil marks.

There are two kinds of rubber: natural and synthetic. *Natural rubber* comes from *latex*, a fluid produced by the rubber tree (Hevea brasiliensis). *Synthetic rubber* is made from chemicals.

For years, virtually all of the world's rubber came from trees growing wild in the rain-forests of Brazil, the original home of the rubber tree. In 1876, some seeds were sent to England and used to start plantations in Malaya and the East Indies. Today almost all natural rubber comes from South-East Asia.

Rubber is gathered from the tree by *tapping*—cutting sloping grooves in the bark. The latex oozes out into a cup attached to the tree below the cuts. The latex is collected and strained to remove dirt and twigs. Then acid is added to coagulate it into solid rubber. This *crude* rubber is pressed into bales and sent to market.

Artificial rubber was discovered in Germany in the 1930's. It is a kind of plastic, and is made by heating simple chemicals together so that complex products form with properties like those of natural rubber.

Crude rubber both from the plantation and the factory has to be treated before it can be moulded into tyres and other articles. The most important of these treatments is *vulcanizing*, in which sulphur is added to the rubber in order to strengthen it.

Talking points
* Describe the different processes that rubber has to go through from the time that it is collected from the tree to when it becomes a tyre on a motor car.
* List the many uses of rubber. Can you think of any other substance that has as many different properties and functions as rubber?
* Find out about the history of rubber. Who were the first people to use it? How did it spread from South America to the rest of the world? Who discovered its various uses? How did synthetic rubber come to be invented?
Articles to read
Adhesives; Malaya.

Ruhr is a region in northern West Germany that has become the greatest industrial area in Europe. The Ruhr district lies east of the River Rhine between two of its tributaries, the Ruhr in the south and the Lippe in the north.

The cities of the Ruhr are heavily populated and so close together that they form a continuous belt. They include Duisburg on the Rhine, Essen and Dortmund in the west. Many railway lines and roads link the cities and a system of canals provides connections with other waterways in Germany and the Netherlands.

Immense coalfields of hard, coking coal are the basis of the region's prosperity. The coal powers giant furnaces that convert iron ore into steel. The steel then goes into heavy machinery and engineering products. The manufacture of chemicals and oil-refining are other major industries.

The development of the Ruhr valley began in the 1800's. Iron mines in Lorraine (won from France in 1871) supplied the raw materials until World War I, after which Swedish ore was used. During World War II the factories of Krupps and other companies in the Ruhr supplied the German forces with essential armaments. The Allies laid waste huge areas of the Ruhr with repeated heavy bombing raids.

After the war, industries were rebuilt under international control. West Germany's post-war prosperity was largely due to the speed with which the Ruhr regained its industrial importance.

Above: Bucharest, the capital city of Rumania, has a modern appearance. Most of its ancient buildings have been destroyed over the years by earthquakes.
Left: Location map of Rumania.
Below: Much of Rumania's farmland has been organized into large collective farms, but a lot remains divided into peasant holdings and is farmed largely without the benefits of mechanization.

Rumania is a rugged country in south eastern Europe. It has a short coastline facing the Black Sea. Its neighbours are Russia, Hungary, Yugoslavia and Bulgaria. Rumania is also called Roumania or Romania.

The great Danube River flows along much of Rumania's southern frontier with Bulgaria. Its waters empty into the Black Sea. The plains north of the Danube and along the coast are well-watered and very fertile. The Transylvanian Alps sweep across the country from west to east, curving northwards to join the Carpathian Mountains. In summer, most of Rumania is hot with a moderate rainfall, but snow blankets the country in winter.

Most Rumanians are farmers or farm workers. But about a third of the people live in cities and towns. Rumanians speak a language derived from Latin. Most people are Christians, belonging to the Rumanian Orthodox Church. But some Rumanians are Jews, Muslims, or Roman Catholics.

Rumanian farmers grow many crops, including fruit, maize, sugar-beet and wheat. They also rear cattle and sheep. Most farmland is organized in huge collective farms, where hundreds of people work. Fishermen catch sturgeon, from which they obtain caviar, a roe which is considered a delicacy throughout the world. Rumanians are skilful at embroidery and weave fine rugs.

The country has thick forests in the mountains and plenty of fish in the rivers. Rumania has large reserves of natural gas and petroleum. Petroleum is piped from the rich oil fields of Constanta, on the Black Sea. Rumania trades mainly with communist countries, including Russia.

Rumania became completely independent by 1878. It became a communist country after the end of World War II. Russian soldiers were stationed in the country until 1958. In the 1950's and 1960's, heavy industry was expanded.

Facts and Figures:
Area: 91,699 square miles.
Population: 20,800,000.
Capital: Bucharest.

Ruminants are animals with *cloven* (split) hoofs, and a system of eating and digestion known as *chewing the cud*. Most ruminants have four cavities in the stomach. These are the *rumen* or paunch, the *reticulum*, the *omasum*, and the *abomasum*. A half-chewed mouthful of food is swallowed and passes down to the rumen, where it is partly digested. It goes on from there to the reticulum, where it is softened and formed into small masses called *cud*. The cud is sent back to the animal's mouth, where it is thoroughly chewed again, and mixed with saliva.

The cud is swallowed once more, passing through the rumen and reticulum to the omasum and abomasum, where stomach juices complete the process of digestion. Well known ruminants are sheep, cows, goats, deer and oxen.

Russian Revolution was one of the major historical events of the 20th century. It released the peasants and workers of Russia from the tyrannical, often cruel. rule of the czars and established the world's first communist government. After the revolution, industries were nationalized and land and property were removed from private ownership. But the new government became another dictatorship.

Although unrest had been building up in Russia for many years, the revolution itself began accidentally in January 1905. A group of workers who had come to the palace of Czar Nicholas II in St. Petersburg, to complain about lack of food and other grievances, were fired on by palace guards. *Bloody Sunday,* as this day was called, started a wave of riots, strikes and demonstrations. The czar authorized a few improvements, including a law-making *Duma* (parliament) with limited powers. The revolutionaries formed their own ouncil or *soviet* in exile.

The next important events came in 1917, a time when Russia was suffering greatly from defeats in World War I. In March (February by the old Russian calendar), a series of strikes broke out in Petrograd (the new name for St. Petersburg) among dissatisfied workers. Soldiers and housewives soon joined them. The people forced the czar to abdicate, and a provisional government was established, under Alexander Kerensky.

In 1917 workers gathered in the cold winter streets of Moscow to listen to Revolutionary speakers.

Lenin, the leader of the *Bolsheviks* (radical wing of the communists who followed the teachings of Karl Marx), returned from exile and began to gain power in the revolutionary soviet. Finally, in November (October by the Russian calendar), he and Leon Trotsky led a successful armed revolt against Kerensky's government and Lenin became leader. During the next few years, the communist government, called the Reds, fought a civil war against the anti-communists, or Whites. The Reds won and became the undisputed leaders of the country. After 1922 Russia became known as the Union of Soviet Socialist Republics.

Rutherford, Ernest (1871-1937), a British physicist, is regarded as the father of atomic science. He established the basic structure of the *atom* as a heavy, positively-charged *nucleus* (central mass) with negatively-charged electrons spinning around it. He discovered *protons* (one component of the nucleus), and predicted the existence of *neutrons* (the other component). Rutherford explored basic properties of *radioactivity,* such as the fact that there are three types of radioactive *emission* (giving out), namely *alpha, beta* and *gamma* particles. He discovered that radioactive substances change in structure as a result of their emission; and that atoms can be smashed by radioactive bombardment. Rutherford won the 1908 Nobel Prize in chemistry.

Rutherford was born in New Zealand, and studied there and at Cambridge University. He later became professor of physics at Cambridge. He was knighted in 1914 and became a life peer in 1932.

Rutland, with an area of only 152 square miles, is the smallest county in England. Its county town is Oakham, and its population is 27,500.

Rutland is a rural county of rolling hills and stone-built villages. It is drained by

1149

the Chater and the Welland, which flows along the southern border with Northamptonshire. Farming is the main occupation. Sheep are bred on the western uplands and beef and dairy farms thrive on the fine grassland. About half the farming area is under cultivation. The main crops are barley, wheat, oats and root crops. Rutland is also noted for its production of Stilton cheese. Its Cottesmore Hunt has a national reputation.

Rwanda is a densely populated country in east-central Africa. It has an area of 10,169 square miles, and a population of over 3,600,000. It is one of the poorest of the African countries. The Rwandans are mainly Bantu-speaking. The Bahutu tribe is the largest. Its members are farmers. The tall Watusi people ruled the area for centuries. The Watusi are by tradition herders.

Rwanda's neighbours are Uganda, Tanzania, Burundi and Zaïre. Much of the country is high and mountainous. The climate is cool and pleasant. Forests which once covered much of the country have been cut down for farmland. Coffee is the chief export crop. The country also mines tin and wolfram (tungsten ore). Kigali, the capital, is the largest town.

Europeans began to colonize Rwanda and neighbouring Burundi (then known together as Ruanda-Urundi) in the 1800's. It became a Belgian territory after World

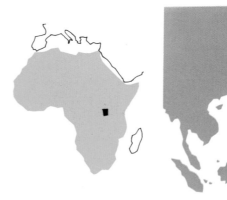

Left: The map shows the location of Rwanda in Africa.

Right: The map shows the location of the Ryukyu Islands in the Pacific.

War I. In 1962 Rwanda and Burundi became separate and independent countries.

Ryukyu Islands lie in the western Pacific Ocean. They form a 650-mile-long chain between Formosa and the islands of Japan. Okinawa is the largest and most important island in the group. The Ryukyu Islands are mountainous and volcanic. Their 1,183,000 people farm or fish for a living. They grow rice and sweet potatoes, and export sugar-cane and pineapples. The United States took the islands from Japan after World War II. The islands were returned in 1972.

S

Sabah is a state of East Malaysia. It was formerly the British colony of *North Borneo*. Situated in north-eastern Borneo, Sabah occupies an area of 29,388 square miles. Most of the state consists of high, forest-covered mountains. Mangrove swamps make up a thin coastal strip. Sabah's climate is hot and humid, with abundant rainfall. Besides timber (the

A woman of the Watusi people of Rwanda. The tall Watusi make up about 14 per cent of Rwanda's people.

leading export) rubber and coconuts are also exported. Many of the inhabitants live by tending rice fields. Dusuns and other native groups make up most of Sabah's population of 656,000. Jesselton is the capital and largest town.

The British North Borneo Company leased much of the area of Sabah from the ruling sultans in 1877 and 1878, and bought the rest from the Austrian consul-general at Hong Kong. Several years later, Britain granted the company a charter to rule. North Borneo became a Crown colony in 1946. In 1963, it joined the newly formed Federation of Malaysia.

Safety means preventing accidents where-ever they may occur—at home, at work, on the road or in recreation areas. Today, national organizations, such as Britain's Royal Society for the Prevention of Acci-dents, exist in many countries to see that accident rates are cut. Such organizations stress the three E's of safety: Engineering, Enforcement and Education.

Engineering means designing buildings that are well-lighted and fireproof, and equipment that will not cut, catch, burn, crush or otherwise injure the user.

Dangerous machines and appliances usually have guard rails, warning lights, automatic cut-off switches and other built-in safety features. Where possible, the most dangerous industrial operations have been made automatic, so that workers need not be endangered at all.

Enforcement means seeing that safety laws are passed and then obeyed. The first of such laws came into effect during the Industrial Revolution, when dangers became obvious in factories and mines. Although such laws have been strength-ened over the years, some companies still endanger their workers by ignoring the safeguards. Car accidents have led some countries to demand seat belts and other safety devices in new cars. The highway code outlines the rules of the road.

Education involves teaching people the precautions and common-sense rules of safety. Some important rules are: Do not touch electrical wires with wet hands; do not go swimming immediately after a meal; and do not leave poisons where children can reach them.

Below: Safety precautions and risks. Helmets and seat belts ensure safer travel. Hazards in the home: Unguarded fires, saucepan handles, ladders and upturned rakes.

Sahara The world's largest desert, the Sahara, covers about three million square miles of northern Africa. It extends from the coast of the Atlantic Ocean in the west to the Red Sea in the east.

The Sahara includes parts of Algeria, Chad, Egypt, Libya, Mali, Mauritania, Morocco, Spanish Sahara, Sudan and Tunisia. Sand dunes, which are constantly shifted by the wind, cover about a third of the desert. The rest consists of upland areas of bare rock, called *hammada,* and regions covered by gravel or stones. Some windswept depressions are several hundred feet below sea level.

Three main mountain regions rise from the Sahara—the Ahaggar of southern Algeria, the Air of northern Nigeria and the Tibesti mountains of northern Chad. The highest peaks, which rise from the Tibesti range, reach more than 11,000 feet above sea-level.

Sand dunes cover one-third of the Sahara. The rest consists of rocky uplands (top left) and gravelly plains. Despite the hostile conditions, people have made their homes in the Sahara since ancient times, Some wander the desert with their animals. Others live in the oases where springs and wells provide water for crops and a resting place for the camel caravans which were once the sole means of transport across the desert (above). Recently, large deposits of natural gas and petroleum have been discovered. The picture (left) shows blast holes being bored in rocky ground along a pipeline route in Libya. Drilling has also revealed the presence of large underground lakes which may bring a greater change to the desert way of life than the discovery of oil.

with the ancient Negro empires that lay to the south.

In the 1950's and 1960's, geologists discovered huge reserves of petroleum and natural gas under the Sahara, especially in Algeria and Libya. Other minerals found in the Sahara include coal, copper, iron ore and phosphates. The geologists also located great underground reservoirs of water, which can be pumped to the surface, turning the shifting sands into fertile farmland.

Saigon is the capital and largest city of the Republic of Vietnam (South Vietnam). Together with its twin city of Cholon, predominantly a Chinese quarter, it covers an area of 51 square miles, with a total population of 2 million. It is situated on the Saigon River to the east of the Mekong delta, 60 miles from the coast of the South China Sea. The city is the seat of government and the main administrative and commercial centre. It is also South Vietnam's major port.

Saigon was the chief city of the French colonial empire of Indo-China. It still has a French atmosphere to it, although the Americans have also influenced it since their involvement in the Vietnam war.

Sailing is the art of handling a vessel equipped with canvas extended on spars, the force of the wind acting on the spread of canvas as the means of propulsion. Skilfully handled, a boat under sail can go in any direction except right into the wind.

Since the seventeenth century, racing has taken place for sailing vessels of many different classes, ranging from the 'J' class cutters which once raced for the America's Cup—135 feet overall, with a 20 foot beam, displacing about 170 tons, and with a sail area of nearly 8,000 square feet—to the small dinghy raced today on inland waters.

The first recorded race between yachts in England was in Pepys Diary for October 1, 1661 as a £100 stake race between

Above: The billowing multi-coloured sail is called a spinnaker. This is hoisted on a special boom and is often used by racing yachts as an extra jib when running before the wind.

Right: When the wind is not blowing directly along the correct course the yacht tends to heel over, and the crew may have to lean over the side in order to avoid capsizing.

The intense heat—summer temperatures sometimes reach 118°F (48°C)—the blinding sandstorms and the lack of surface water make the Sahara unattractive to most people. But people live in the fertile Nile valley and around *oases,* where springs or wells provide water for farming. Apricots, barley, date palms, maize, oranges, pomegranates, vines and wheat all flourish around oases.

Since ancient times, Arab, Berber and Tuareg peoples of the Sahara have been nomads, who roamed the desert from one oasis to another with their livestock. Merchants from northern Africa crossed the Sahara in camel caravans, trading

1153

Charles II and his brother, the Duke of York, over 23 miles from Greenwich to Gravesend.

The Royal Cork Yacht Club was established in 1720 and the Royal Thames Yacht Club in 1775. The Royal Yacht Squadron organized racing for large powerful vessels from 1815, and in 1823 the Royal Yacht Club, also based at Cowes, started to organize regular races for small vessels.

The America's Cup races, open to challenge by any nation, began in 1870. So far, U.S.A. holders have never been defeated. One of the toughest ocean yacht races is the Sydney to Hobart race. This is over a course of 680 miles and takes about four days. It traditionally starts on Boxing Day every year.

Yachting was first added to the Olympic Games at the beginning of this century, and six classes were raced in 1972—

Soling, Dragon, Star, Tempest, Flying Dutchman and Finn. Paul Elvstrøm (Denmark) won yachting gold medals in four successive Olympics from 1948-1960. Elvstrøm had also won eight other world titles in six different classes.

St. John's, capital, chief port, and industrial centre of the Canadian province of Newfoundland, is one of the oldest continuously occupied cities of North America. Its population is 91,000.

St. John's is built on a fine, natural, sheltered harbour on the east coast of the Avalon Peninsula. The entrance to the harbour is flanked by cliffs more than 500 feet high. The port serves Atlantic trade and the fishing industry. There are large factories for fish processing and packing, and for the refining of whale and seal oil.

John Cabot is believed to have discovered the harbour in 1497, and Sir Humphrey Gilbert founded the town in 1582. English and French rivalry over the port was settled in 1713 by the Treaty of Utrecht, which ceded Newfoundland to England.

St. Helena is a barren, rocky island in the south Atlantic Ocean, belonging to Britain. The island covers an area of 47 square miles and has 5,000 inhabitants. Jamestown is the capital and only town. Flax, from which lace and rope are made, is the leading crop. The island was formerly a stopping place for ships that sailed round Africa. Discovered by the Portuguese in 1502, it was acquired by Britain in 1659, and made a colony in 1834. Napoleon Bonaparte spent his last years in exile on St. Helena.

St. Lawrence River This river is now the final link in the great water system which, including the Great Lakes and the St. Louis River, extends 2,480 miles from Belle Isle at the entrance to the Atlantic to the heart of Minnesota.

The St. Lawrence issues from the

Since the St. Lawrence Seaway was opened in 1959, deep draft shipping has been able to penetrate 2,480 miles into the heart of North America. Inland cities have been transformed into thriving ports handling ever increasing tonnages of cargo.

eastern end of Lake Ontario, and its steep and broken descent is marked by many rapids. It is bordered to the north by Canada and to the south by the United States.

The river was discovered in 1535 by a Frenchman, Jacques Cartier, and was used to further the fur trade. With the later development of North America, particularly the Canadian north-west, the St. Lawrence assumed new importance as a great avenue of trade with Europe.

The St. Lawrence valley is the main east-west axis of the Canadian transportation system. And owing to the use of hydro-electric power developed as part of the St. Lawrence Seaway project, it is also the industrial heart of the country.

The St. Lawrence Seaway project was the subject of controversy for more than half a century, and although it was first agreed on by Canada and the United States in 1921, it was not until 1959 that it was officially opened by Queen Elizabeth II and President Eisenhower.

Part of the project was the deepening of a ship channel from Montreal to the head of the Great Lakes. As a result, ports as far inland as the lake-head are now open to deep-sea shipping, and it also allows the shipment of coal, iron ore, timber and grain.

As the second main part of the project, the many rapids, particularly in the Niagara and Beauharnois areas, have been harnessed to provide hydro-electric power. This power is available to the main industrial centres of southern Ontario and upper New York.

Saints are holy people. To become a Christian saint, a man or woman must satisfy certain conditions. The process is known as *canonization*. The Roman Catholic Church examines claims to canonization carefully. A commission goes through every aspect of the person's life

---

Uccello's painting of St. George and the dragon has done much to keep alive the legend of England's patron saint.

to ensure that he was entirely good, and had the power to perform miracles.

Most saints are canonized many years after their death. They are usually *beatified* (pronounced blessed) as a first stage. Saints who lived before the year A.D. 1000 are accepted purely through their traditional holiness. Many saints died as martyrs, or were crucified, burnt, or even torn to pieces by wild animals.

Most trades and professions have their patron saints. For example, St. Helen is the patron saint of dyers, St. Thomas More of lawyers, St. Francis Xavier of missionaries, St. Thomas Aquinas of scholars, St. Crispin of shoemakers, and St. Clare of television. St. Clare, when on her death-bed, saw a vision of the Mass that was being sung a mile and a half away. In 1958 the pope declared her the patron saint of television, which can bring the Mass to the bed-ridden. Many countries also have patron saints. For example, St. George is the patron saint of England, St. David of Wales, St. Andrew of Scotland, and St. Patrick of Ireland. In 1969 the Roman Catholic Church reviewed the list of saints. Some of the traditional saints were taken off the list because it was thought that there was not enough evidence that they were worthy enough. Among them was St. Christopher. In 1970, the Pope announced that the 40 Martyrs, who had suffered in Britain in the period between the Reformation and the Act of Catholic Emancipation, had been canonized.

Some people venerate bones and other relics of saints, which they believe have miraculous powers. Thousands of sick people flock to Lourdes in France, seeking cures through the intercession of St. Bernadette, who saw a vision of the Virgin Mary there. Mary, the mother of Jesus, is the holiest of all the saints. Roman Catholics venerate her.

Salamanders are amphibian animals related to newts. Salamanders can live both in water and on land. They usually prefer to stay on land, living in moist places on snails and insects. They are mostly small, brightly coloured, lizard-like creatures, but the giant salamander of Japan grows to a length of six feet. Salamanders develop from aquatic larvae into air-breathing adults in the same way as newts. One salamander, the axolotl, normally never reaches the adult stage and breeds while in the larval stage. But by stimulating the thyroid gland, it can be made to change into an adult.

Salmon This is a food fish with an unusual life history. Salmon hatch from eggs laid in quiet inland streams. They spend their adult life in the sea, and return to their birthplaces to breed.

There are two kinds of salmon. The Atlantic salmon breeds in the rivers of western Europe and eastern North America. Pacific salmon breed inland in western North America and eastern Asia. The average weight of an Atlantic salmon is 15 pounds. Pacific salmon vary from 3 to 90 pounds.

The fire salamander is a poisonous creature, but, like the wasp, its conspicuous markings warn potential attackers of the danger. The poison, called salamandrin, is secreted from pores behind its eyes and, although it is not as harmful as it is reputed to be, it can kill a small mammal.

Stages in the Development of a Salmon

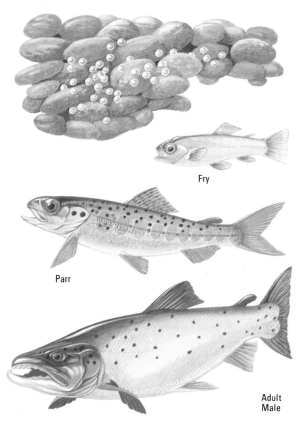

Fry

Parr

Adult
Male

Left: The salmon lays its eggs in the headwaters of rivers. The creature that hatches from the eggs is a larva, called a fry, which begins to feed after a month or so. When the fry has grown to over an inch long it is called a parr. The parr lives in rivers for about two years. After this time it becomes a silvery colour (and is called a smolt) and swims down the river until it reaches the sea, where it becomes an adult salmon.

Below; Salmon return from the sea to freshwater streams to spawn. To do so they have to travel against the flow of the river, and jump rapids and falls. By the time they reach their destination they are worn out and thin, and have lost their bright colour. Once they have laid their eggs they usually die. Here, a salmon leaps high out of the water in an effort to pass the rapids.

Salmon gather in pairs in the spring or autumn to breed, after an exhausting journey far up river from the sea. The female salmon scoops out a shallow hole in the gravel on the stream bed and lays her eggs in it. The male fertilizes the eggs, and the female covers them with a layer of gravel. The parents then drift away from the nest to die, exhausted. All Pacific salmon die after spawning, but a few Atlantic salmon survive to return and breed again.

The young salmon hatch after 10 weeks, and stay around the spawning ground for a year. They then swim down to the sea, where they stay for several years. One day they start back to the inland rivers. Salmon will journey thousands of miles back to their birthplace.

Salt We normally think of 'salt' only as the substance we use for seasoning and preserving food. But to a chemist

'salt' means a lot more. A salt is a chemical compound formed (together with water) when an acid and a base react together. For example, hydrochloric acid combines with sodium hydroxide (base) to form sodium chloride. This is the compound we call *salt*. It is the commonest of the salts and lends its name to all of the others.

Sodium chloride, together with many other salts, is found in sea water. It also occurs in the Earth's crust in massive form as the mineral *halite,* or *rock salt.* Our common table salt comes from one or other of these sources. To remain healthy, all animals must eat a certain amount of salt. That is why farmers feed a 'salt lick' to their cattle.

Sodium chloride is a valuable raw material for industry. For example, caustic soda (for making soap, paper, and rayon) and chlorine (for purifying water, bleaching) are obtained by passing electricity

1157

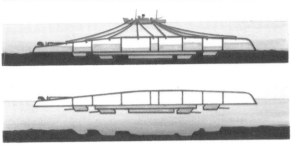

Above: Raising a sunken ship by compressed air.
The ship is filled with compressed air (top) to empty it
of water, making the total weight of the wreck less than
the total weight of the water it displaces. The
displaced water exerts an upward force and the
buoyant wreck is raised to the surface, bottom up
(bottom). Below: Righting a ship sunk in shallow water
by buoyancy and counterweighting.
Pontoons are attached to the wreck: (A) air-filled,
(B) water-filled. Selected compartments (C) are filled
with compressed air. The ship can then be winched into
an upright position.

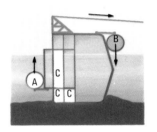

1

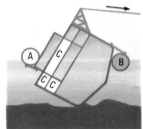

2

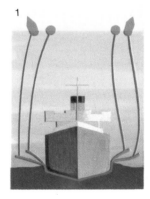

3

Lifting a wreck.
1. Thick wire ropes are
passed under the
vessel and attached to
buoys.
2. At low tide the
wires are made fast to
lifting tugs.
3. At high tide the
wreck lifts off the
bottom and is towed to
shallower water until it
grounds again.
The operation is repeated
at successive high
tides and is thus
gradually moved to
shallow water.

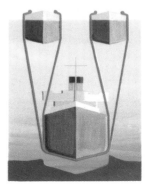

through salt solution, or *brine*. Soda ash
(for making glass) is also obtained by
treating brine.

Just as hydrochloric acid combines
with sodium hydroxide to form sodium
chloride, sulphuric and nitric acids
combine with it to form sodium sulphate
and nitrate. The chloride, sulphate, and
nitrate are the salts of sodium, a metal.
Most metals form salts of this kind.
Carbonates and *phosphates* are other
common salts. Chalk and limestone, for
example, are calcium carbonate. The
most important non-metal to form salts
is ammonia. Its salts are valuable fertilizers.

Salvage Disasters happen at sea even in
this age of echo-sounding and radar.
Saving or recovering ships or their cargo
is called *salvage*. The money paid to the
salvors, the people who carry out the
operation, is also called *salvage*.

In the case of towing a crippled ship,
no salvage is paid until the ship is safely
back in port. If the salvors fail in their
attempts, they get no pay. Salvage is
often dangerous too, because men may
have to go aboard a vessel that threatens
to heel over at any instant. But the re-
wards of success can be great.

When a ship sinks with a valuable cargo,
the salvage experts are again called for.
If the sea is too deep, there is little that
can be done. But recovery down to about
400 feet may well be possible by deep-
sea divers or skin divers if the water is
shallower.

If the ship is not badly damaged, the
salvage crew may try to refloat it. Divers
first repair the damaged hull. Then they
may pump air into it from the surface
until it rises. Or else they may try to lift
it with wires slung between two floating
pontoons.

However, the most exciting salvage
work of all is concerned not with the
present but with the past. For several
thousand years ships have been sink-
ing to the bottom of the seas, taking

with them fabulous treasures and relics of their age. The Caribbean Sea, for example, is littered with the wrecks of Spanish galleons sunk two or three hundred years ago. Quite a few of them have been found. Gold and silver, jewellery, coins, and weapons worth a fortune in cash and in archaeological knowledge have been salvaged.

Salvation Army is a world-wide organization dedicated to charitable work and the spreading of *evangelical Christianity* (emphasizing salvation through faith in Christ). Its founder, William Booth, was an English Methodist minister, who with his wife began preaching at open-air meetings to the people of London's East End, in 1865. The organization's name was changed from the *Christian Mission* to the *Salvation Army* in 1878. The Army gradually grew and spread to the United States, Canada, Australia, India and other countries. Today, it is a vast organization with headquarters in London.

The Salvation Army runs a wide variety of welfare services, such as hospitals and nursing homes; soup kitchens and hostels for the poor; and help for alcoholics, ex-convicts and other less fortunate people. The services are supported by donations of money and goods which the Army sells in special shops. Religious services, with an emphasis on singing and band music, are held regularly.

Salvation Army members wear uniforms and the organization is run on military lines. The lowest rank is that of a *soldier*. Officers are promoted up to *general*. Strict discipline and firm religious belief are required of all Army members.

Samoa is a group of 16 islands in the South Pacific Ocean with a total area of 1,173 square miles. The islands are mountainous and have volcanic soil. The climate is tropical with abundant rainfall. The people of Samoa are Polynesians.

'The church on the kerbside' – people gather round a Salvation Army band and preachers.

Samoa is divided politically into two parts. The western islands of Samoa form the independent country of Western Samoa. It has 131,000 inhabitants. The largest islands are Savai'i and Upolu. Apia, the capital and chief seaport, is on Upola. Western Samoa belonged to Germany from 1900 to 1914. Then New Zealand administered it. It became independent in 1962. Bananas and coconut meat are its leading exports. It is a member of the Commonwealth.

The eastern islands in the group comprise American Samoa, a territory of the United States. The U.S. acquired these islands in 1900. Swains Island was added in 1925. American Samoa has 28,000 people. Its main island is Tutuila.

San Francisco (pop. 715,000) is a city of the state of California, in the United States. It is also an important seaport, well situated on a peninsula enclosing San Francisco Bay on the Pacific coast. The Golden Gate Bridge, which spans the entrance to the bay, is a marvel of engineering. It has one of the longest suspension-type spans in the world. The city is the chief financial centre of the West, and has educational, scientific and cultural institutions. It is the seat of the University of California, which has over 100,000 students. Much of the city has been rebuilt since an earthquake in 1906.

San Marino is a tiny and very old republic, completely enclosed in Italy. It sits astride the triple peaks of Mount Titano near the Adriatic Sea in the Apennine Range, and covers an area of 24 square miles. Picturesque scenery and centuries-old buildings attract the tourist trade. Postage stamps for collectors, quarried building stone and manufactured textiles bring in additional money. Many of the country's 19,000 inhabitants cultivate the land to produce wheat and wine. The people of San Marino speak Italian.

Marinus, a Christian stonecutter fleeing from the Roman emperor Diocletian, is said to have founded the country in the 4th century A.D.

San Martin, José de (1778-1850) was an Argentine general who helped win South America's independence. He was educated in Spain where he fought against Napoleon, but he returned to Argentina in 1812 and joined the revolutionaries. In 1817 he led an army over the Andes into Chile, and despite tremendous hardships defeated the Spaniards at Chacabuco, establishing the independence of Chile. Four years later he captured Lima and declared Peru independent.

In 1822 he relinquished his leadership to Bolivar, another revolutionary, and retired from military life. He died in France in 1850.

A San Francisco street slopes steeply down to the sea. Travelling along it is one of the city's famous cable cars.

Sardinia has a rugged coastline with many small sandy bays.

Sarawak is the largest state of Malaysia. It occupies an area of 48,300 square miles on the northern coast of Borneo. Kalimantan (Indonesian Borneo) lies to the south of it. Sarawak's interior is mountainous, with forests which yield timber for export. Many swift rivers provide transport to the swampy coastal region. Sarawak produces and refines oil. Its farmers grow rice for food, as well as rubber and pepper for export. The busiest port is Kuching, the state capital. Varied groups make up the state's population of 977,000: Sea Dyaks, Chinese, Malays and Land Dyaks are the main groups.

This map shows the location of Sarawak.

Sarawak was ruled for a century by white rajahs, after the ruling sultan of Brunei granted the area to Sir James Brooke in 1841 in return for Brooke's help in putting down a native rebellion. It became a British Crown colony in 1946, then joined the Federation of Malaysia in 1963.

Sardinia, a large island in the Mediterranean Sea, is part of Italy. North of Sardinia is the French island of Corsica. To the east, across the Tyrrhenian Sea lies the mainland of Italy. Sardinia, with its several offshore islands, covers an area of 9,301 square miles. The region has its own lawmaking Assembly. Cagliari is the capital and leading port. Altogether, about 1,450,000 people live in Sardinia.

Because of the rough, mountainous nature of the land, its poor soil and climate, and a history of malaria epidemics, Sardinia remains one of Italy's poorest and least developed regions. The

1161

people live by herding goats and sheep; growing almonds, wine grapes, cereals and olives on the small plains; and by catching tunny and other fish. Some zinc, lead and coal are mined.

Sardinia was inhabited by prehistoric Bronze Age people who built stone structures called *nuraghi*. The Carthaginians, Romans, and many other groups conquered the islands at various times. The kingdom of Sardinia, founded in 1720, was ruled by the House of Savoy. It became part of a united Italy in 1861.

Sargasso Sea is a region of the north Atlantic Ocean, lying north-east of the West Indies. Its name comes from beds of *Sargassum* (gulf-weed) that drifts on its usually calm surface. The waters of the Sargasso Sea are exceptionally blue, clear and salty. Many unusual forms of animal life inhabit the region, including some normally found close to the shore. Christopher Columbus sailed across the Sargasso Sea on his first voyage to the New World.

Saskatchewan is one of Canada's grain-producing Prairie Provinces. Its farmlands supply three-fifths of the country's total crop of wheat. Saskatchewan's industries, especially mining, are growing rapidly.

Saskatchewan borders on Alberta in the west, the Northwest Territories in the north, Manitoba in the east, and the United States in the south. Its area is

Location map of Saskatchewan. Its huge wheat output has earned it the nickname Canada's Bread-basket.

251,700 square miles. Its climate is cold in winter and warm in summer. Northern Saskatchewan is largely uninhabited. The land is rocky, rich in minerals, and covered with evergreen forests. Fur-bearing animals inhabit the woods. The many lakes and streams are filled with fish.

Most of Saskatchewan's 943,000 inhabitants live in the southern plains. In this region are the farmlands—comprising a third of Canada's total agricultural area. The cities are also in the south. Regina, the provincial capital, is the largest city. It has many factories and refineries. Saskatoon is the second largest city. It is the marketing centre for the province's farm products.

Since the 1950's, the petroleum industry has become important. Oil is produced in the province and also refined there. Potash, used in making fertilizers, has also become important in recent years. So has uranium. Among Saskatchewan's other valuable minerals are copper, gold, natural gas and zinc.

Saskatchewan's factories produce pulp and paper from the province's timber. Cement, chemicals, processed food and electrical equipment are manufactured as well.

Besides wheat, Saskatchewan's farmers grow other cereals including barley, oats and rye. They raise beef and dairy cattle.

The Cree, Assiniboin, and Chipewyan Indians were Saskatchewan's first inhabitants. In 1670, Charles II of England granted fur trading rights in the region to the Hudson's Bay Company. In 1690, Henry Kelsey of the company became the first European to explore the region. Trading settlements were soon established. In 1870 Saskatchewan became a territory within the Dominion of Canada. It became a province in 1905.

Satellites The Earth and the other planets form the main part of the Sun's 'family', or *solar system.* They move in great oval paths, or *orbits,* around the Sun. Many of the planets also have their

Weather satellites are able to transmit pictures of cloud formations back to earth and give advance warning of storms. The mosaic (above) built up from photographs taken by the satellite Essa 5 shows eight major storm centres in the northern hemisphere in a single day, including hurricane Beulah (bottom centre) which subsequently caused damage amounting to billions of dollars in the Caribbean.

own 'family' of orbiting bodies, which are called *satellites*.

The Earth, for example, has only one satellite — the Moon. But Jupiter has twelve satellites, Saturn ten, Uranus five, Mars two, and Neptune two.

The Earth now also has a large number of artificial satellites. They are the spacecraft that scientists have launched into space for various purposes. Russia's launching of the first artificial satellite, Sputnik 1, on 4th October, 1957, marked the beginning of the Space Age. (See Astronautics; Space probes.)

Scientific satellites are sent into space to measure such things as the Earth's magnetism and radiation coming from the Sun or from outer space.

Weather satellites have television cameras trained on the Earth which transmit pictures of cloud formations in the atmosphere. Scientists can tell from these photographs how and where our weather begins. They can warn people in advance about storms and hurricanes.

Above: Satellites are normally powered by solar batteries. These consist of small cells made of silicon. When sunlight falls on each silicon cell, a small electric current is produced. The cells may be arranged around the outside surface of the satellite, or on 'paddles' which extend like wings from the sides of the craft. Below: A satellite orbiting 22,300 miles above the equator will circle the Earth once every twenty-four hours. It will therefore appear to be stationary in the sky. This is important for communications satellites which can be 'positioned' as required in the sky.

Communications satellites relay television programmes, and telephone and telegraph messages around the world. The latest ones can handle several programmes and hundreds of messages all at the same time. They have their own receiver and transmitter, powered by batteries charged by the Sun's rays. The satellites receive a signal from the transmitting station, amplify it, and beam

1163

strong signals back to the receiving station.

Early communications satellites, such as Telstar (1962), circle constantly around the Earth. They are in contact with ground stations for only part of the time. But the latest satellites are put into a stationary, or *synchronous* orbit 22,300 miles above the Equator. They rotate once in the same time (24 hours) as it takes the Earth to rotate. They therefore appear to be stationary.

Saturn is the second largest planet of the Solar System. It is the only planet with a system of rings around it. To the naked eye, Saturn looks like a bright yellow star. It travels round the Sun in a path lying between those of Jupiter and Uranus.

Saturn is so far from the Sun that it takes 29½ Earth-years to circle it once. Saturn revolves on its axis more than twice as fast as the Earth, so that each day is only 10¼ hours long. There can be no life as we know it on Saturn, because it is so cold (minus 155°C.).

Saturn is much bigger than the Earth. Its surface area is about 80 times as large, but it is made up mostly of lighter material, so the Earth is 8 times as dense as Saturn. If you could place Saturn in water it would float.

Nobody can be certain what Saturn is made of. Some astronomers think that the centre of the planet is probably a small core of rock and metal. Outside this there is probably a deep layer of ice, several

Saturn compared in size with the Earth. The planet is surrounded by three separate rings, which are each made up of many millions of small particles.

Fishing is a thriving industry in Scandinavia and a vast range of sea foods is enjoyed by the people.

thousand miles thick. Surrounding the solid planet is a thick layer of atmosphere, made up of various gases.

Saturn has 10 known moons. The nearest, Janus, is only 98,000 miles from the planet's centre. The largest, Titan, is slightly larger than the planet Mercury and is the biggest moon in the Solar System.

Saturn may once have had another moon, but it is believed to have broken into pieces, which now form the rings. Viewed edge-on, the rings appear as an extremely thin disc, measuring 170,000 miles across but only about 10 miles thick.

Scandinavia is a long peninsula in northern Europe which contains Norway and Sweden. But people often use the term *Scandinavian countries,* which also includes Denmark, Finland and Iceland.

The Scandinavian peninsula is very mountainous in the west. The mountains fall steeply to the Atlantic Ocean and the North Sea. The west coast has many *fjords,* long, narrow sea inlets, and many offshore islands. To the east, the mountains slope down to a plain.

Northern Scandinavia lies north of the Arctic Circle. Important resources of the peninsula include iron ore and timber.

Scavengers are creatures that feed on *carrion* (dead animals) or animal waste

A scarab beetle rolling a ball of dung with its hind legs. An egg laid in the dung develops into a grub that feeds inside the ball (shown cut open).

such as dung. Scavengers are nature's dustmen, getting rid of decaying and dead matter that would otherwise quickly make the whole world a gigantic rubbish dump. Even more important, however, scavengers return to the soil materials vital for plant growth—and thus the food of animals. Without them, for example, the world's supply of nitrogen compounds—a vital part of proteins—would soon be exhausted.

Some of the most useful scavengers are insects, especially beetles and flies. Some beetles and flies lay their eggs on the dead bodies of animals. When the eggs hatch, the larvae have a ready food supply. Other flies and beetles eat and lay their eggs on animal dung.

More spectacular scavengers are the carrion-eating birds and mammals, such as vultures, crows, jackals and hyenas. They quickly dispose of any corpse, whether the animal died naturally or was killed by a hunting animal. More important

Today many schools set up joint groups of parents and teachers. They can talk over the pupils' problems and exchange ideas on how the school programmes could be improved. Pupils, too, are having an increasing say in how they think their schools should be organized.

even than these, however, are the millions upon millions of bacteria and other micro-organisms that complete the breakdown of organic matter.

Schools Nearly all countries in the world try to provide enough schools to give their children some education. In many countries laws are passed by which children have to go to school when they reach a certain age. In Britain this is five; in most other countries it is six. Schools are usually built and run by what are called local authorities. These may be towns and counties as in Britain, or school districts as in the U.S.A. Schools are divided into different types according to the kind of education they provide (see Education). Some children go to nursery school when they are very young. At these schools they learn to play together. At the age of five or six, depending upon the country, children go to primary schools. Modern teaching methods in primary schools encourage the children to be as active as possible and to find out as much as they can for themselves. Some new schools have been

At the end of each term or year schoolchildren sit examinations to test their abilities in the subjects they have studied.

built with a number of working areas in each of which small groups of children can do different kinds of work.

The age at which a boy or girl leaves a primary school varies a good deal from country to country but is often 11 or 12. Pupils then go on to secondary schools. They may go to different types of secondary school. In England, for instance, there have been grammar, technical and modern schools taking pupils of different abilities but these are being replaced by comprehensive schools which take all children in an area. These are often large schools with as many as 2,000 children in them. Many American high schools are of this size too. In secondary schools pupils study a number of different subjects. They may, as they get older, spend more time on fewer subjects. A pupil of 16 to 18 years old may study a group of related subjects such as English, History and Geography, or Chemistry, Physics and Mathematics. Some countries have a wider range of subjects for school pupils. In most cases a pupil's career at secondary school ends with some kind of examination to show his ability in the work he has done. (See Education.)

Scorpion This is a small insect-like animal with a poisonous sting at the end of its flexible, jointed tail. The scorpion is not an insect but an *arachnid,* related to spiders and mites. The scorpion has four pairs of legs, unlike insects, which have three pairs. Behind the head are an extra pair of limbs with large pincers. The tail curves over the back of the scorpion. Scorpions are born alive and cling to their mother's back for the first few days of life.

Scorpions live in the warmer regions of the world. They eat insects and spiders and other small animals, often hunting by night and resting during the day. They seize their prey in their pincers and sometimes kill it with their poison. The sting is more often used in defence. The poison may be dangerous to man. A scorpion sting is very painful but is rarely fatal.

A scorpion lashes out with its pincers to catch a lizard. The sting is rarely used for capturing food.

Scorpions shelter in crevices and under stones and trees. They may also shelter in shoes or clothes. In regions where scorpions are found, shoes and clothes should be shaken out before dressing.

Scotland is a country in western Europe. Covering an area of 30,411 square miles, it is the northern part of the island of Great Britain. It forms part of the United Kingdom (see United Kingdom). The Irish Sea and the Atlantic Ocean lie to the west of Scotland, and the North Sea to the north and east. England borders Scotland to the south. Two groups of islands to the north-east of the country, the Orkneys and the Shetlands, also form part of Scotland.

The northern part of Scotland is mountainous, and is known as the *Highlands.* It covers two-thirds of the country, but only one in ten of the people live there. Many of the mountains are steep and rocky, with deep valleys and lakes, called *lochs.* Ben Nevis (4,406 feet above sea level) is the highest mountain.

The Great Glen, a valley with a chain of lochs in it, runs north-east to south-west. The longest loch is Loch Ness, which is more than 700 feet deep. The soil of the Highlands is poor, and many areas have few trees. Foresters are planting more trees, but agriculture and industry are of little importance. Tourism is an important source of income, and people ski in the Highlands in winter. Streams provide hydro-electric power.

West of the mainland lie the Hebrides, a chain of rocky islands. The Hebrides are well-known for Harris tweed, which is named after one of the islands.

South of the Highlands lie the *Lowlands*, a wide, fertile region. Most of Scotland's farms, industries and large cities lie in this area. Edinburgh, the capital, stands on the Firth of Forth, in the east. Glasgow, the largest city and a centre of engineering and shipbuilding, stands on the River Clyde in the west.

The *Southern Uplands* lie between the Lowlands and the border with England. Most of the hills are flatter than those of the Highlands, and are covered with grass. Farmers graze sheep and cattle on them. The main north-south rail and road

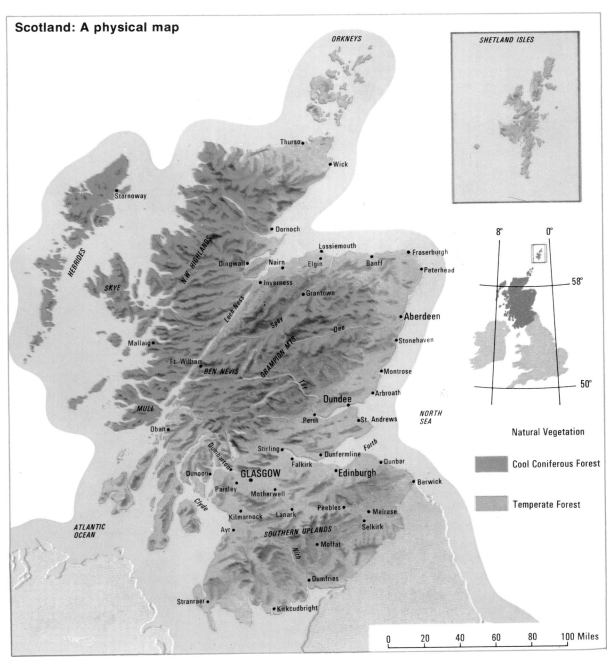

Scotland: A physical map

Natural Vegetation

Cool Coniferous Forest

Temperate Forest

0   20   40   60   80   100 Miles

Above: A team of dancers, dressed in traditional costume, perform Scottish dances at the Conal Games.

Below: Herrings are split, ready to be made into kippers, in a Scottish port.

routes run through narrow valleys in the Southern Uplands.

Most of the 5,228,000 people of Scotland are of Celtic origin. They do not have a separate government, but they have their own system of law and many of their customs differ from those of the rest of the United Kingdom.

Celtic people settled in Scotland about 2,500 years ago. The Romans called them *Picts*. During the Roman occupation of Britain, up to the early A.D. 400's, the Picts remained largely independent.

Before the Romans left, Celts from Ireland, called *Scots,* settled in western Scotland. By the 800's, a Scots king, Kenneth MacAlpine, ruled over both Picts and Scots. Constant warfare went on between Scotland and England.

Trouble flared up in 1290 after a long spell of peace, when the Scots queen Margaret died, and several barons claimed the throne. Edward I of England declared that John Balliol was the rightful king. Many Scots fought against this, and in 1296, Edward claimed the Scottish throne himself.

The Scots, led first by William Wallace and later by Robert Bruce, fought the English until 1328. The English then recognized the independence of Scotland, with Bruce as its king, Robert I.

In 1371, the family of Stuart won the Scottish throne. The Stuarts had violent lives, several of them dying in wars against the English. James IV of Scotland made peace with the English, and married the daughter of Henry VII. But wars soon broke out again. The Scots became allies of the French, who were also enemies of the English.

After the Reformation, religious wars between Protestants and Roman Catholics broke out in the 1500's. The Scots, who were mostly Protestant, drove Mary, Queen of. Scots, from the throne because she was a Roman Catholic. But Mary's son, James VI, succeeded to the throne of England too, in 1603. A hundred years later, in 1707, England and Scotland became one country, with one parliament.

Scott, Robert Falcon (1868-1912), was a British naval officer and Antarctic explorer. He led two important polar expeditions, losing his life on the second one after great heroism.

Scott was born in Plymouth and entered the navy in 1880. In 1901 he sailed in the *Discovery* on his first Antarctic expedition. He spent two summers and a winter on the ice and pioneered a route to the South Pole.

In 1910 Scott set off again for the South Pole. On the way he learned that the Norwegian explorer Roald Amundsen

Opposite: The rugged beauty of the Scottish highlands. The road leads over the Pass of Melfort in Argyllshire.

1168

1169

Scott's own account of the last few days before he and his companions met their deaths can be read in his diaries, which were found beside his body.

had set out for the same destination. Scott established an Antarctic base with ponies, motor-tractors, and dog sledges. His companions were Lieutenant Harry Bowers, Captain Lawrence Oates, Dr. Edward Wilson, and Petty Officer Edgar Evans.

The tractors proved useless, the ponies collapsed, and there were too few dogs. On the last stages the men pulled the sledges themselves. At times the party was completely halted by blizzards. They finally reached the South Pole on the 18th

A group of Scouts sets up camp. Scouts are encouraged to be handy and self-reliant.

January, 1912, only to find that Amundsen had beaten them to it by four weeks.

On the 900-mile return journey, Evans died first. Oates gallantly walked out into the blizzard to his death because he felt that he was delaying his companions. Scott, Bowers, and Wilson died one short march from safety. A relief party found their bodies and diaries.

Scouting is an international movement for boys and girls. It was founded in England in 1907 by Robert Baden-Powell, later Lord Baden-Powell. The organization was originally for boys only. But three years later a similar organization, known as the Girl Guides was founded for girls. The scouting movement grew rapidly in Britain, and soon spread to other countries. Today there are more than 19,000,000 Boy Scouts and Girl Guides (called Girl Scouts in some countries) in the world.

Young children—from the age of 7 or 8 to 11—belong either to Cub Scout or Brownie Guide units. Older children—from about 10 or 11 to 15—become full Scouts or Guides. Youths from the age of 14, 15 or 16 upwards become Venture Scouts or Ranger Guides. Sea Scouts have a special interest in boating. Air Scouts learn about flying.

One aim of scouting is to build character and self-reliance in young people. Another is to teach helpfulness to others.

Scouts pledge themselves to Scout Promise and Scout Law. In addition, scouting has its own motto: 'Be prepared'.

All Scouts learn the basic skills outlined in the Scout handbook. These include building a campfire, administering first-aid, tying knots and reading a compass. Outstanding Scouts are eligible for awards, such as the Queen's Scout award, the highest for boys in Britain.

Scouts and Guides wear special uniforms. These vary from country to country. Scout troops usually have weekly meetings. They may also go on weekend trips, which often include hiking and sleeping out of doors. In addition, many Scouts have the opportunity of going to summer camps. Scouts of different nations come together every four years at an international jamboree.

Sculpture From earliest times and in all parts of the world men have made models and statues, and this art is known as *sculpture*. There are two main methods, the *glyptic* and the *plastic,* from the Greek words meaning *carve* and *mould.*

In the carving method the sculptor takes a block of stone or wood and cuts into it. In the moulding method he starts with a core and builds up his model with pieces of soft clay. Models made in clay usually need to be baked to make them permanent. The resulting model may then be used to make a mould into which concrete, or hot metal (bronze, lead, or silver) is poured.

Carvings have been made in stone of all kinds, and in wood and ivory. In recent times sculptors have resorted to a constructional method—that is, they have built up models and figures out of sheets and bars of metal, and even glass and plastics.

Sculpture can also mean a kind of stone picture known as *relief,* which can be viewed from one position only. By this method, figures or shapes are carved or moulded on a flat base and appear to emerge from their background like a raised picture.

Sculpture has long been used to decorate buildings and to glorify gods or heroes. Many of the statues today represent great leaders of the past. Others depict symbolic figures, such as Eros, the god of love, in Piccadilly Circus in London; the lions at the foot of Nelson's Monument, in London's Trafalgar Square; and the huge Statue of Liberty in New York harbour. Much sculpture is associated with tombs and graves. Because sculpture lasts for many centuries, it is one of our most important sources of knowledge about the past.

Above: These beautiful statues are part of the Erectheum on the Acropolis in Athens.
Right: Michelangelo employed the classical proportions of the Ancient Greeks in his work.

Below: A giant sculpture by Henry Moore outside the Unesco headquarters in Paris.

Until 400 years ago most sculpture was coloured. But artists have come to appreciate uncoloured sculpture, which reveals the natural beauty of the material—the fine texture of stone, the beautiful grain of wood, and so on.

One of the greatest of the later Renaissance period (16th century) sculptures, when the great classical revival was taking place, was the superb statue of *David,* by Michelangelo. It was carved from a piece of marble so large that no other artists had dared to use it. In early classical times the

1171

statue of the god Zeus at Olympia, by Phidias, was one of the wonders of the ancient world.

Sculpture was practised in the earliest days, from Babylon to China, and reached its peak in Europe in Athens, Greece, in 600 B.C. The wonderful Egyptian sculpture, glorifying the pharaohs, was conventional, and Phidias and others freed the art to produce some of the greatest representations of the idealized human figure.

Sculpture then passed through the Romanesque and Gothic periods, to the Great Revival, until at the end of the 19th century the great French sculptor Rodin emerged as one of the world's greatest masters of portraiture. Modern sculptors have since moved more towards abstract (non-representational) figures and groups, and one of the most notable of our day is Henry Moore, some of whose work can be seen in the Tate Gallery, in London.

Sea anemones eat small creatures which they paralyse with their stinging tentacles.

Sea anemone This is a sea animal with a cylindrical body surmounted by a fringe of tentacles around the mouth. It looks somewhat like a flower. Sea anemones attach themselves to rocks and piers on the seashore, and can often be found in tidal pools. They vary in size from a quarter of an inch up to three feet, but common sea anemones are an inch or two in diameter.

The sea anemone uses its tentacles to obtain its food. Any small creature venturing within their reach is paralysed by stinging cells on the tentacles, dragged into the anemone's mouth, and digested.

Sea birds include birds that range the oceans of the world, and those that merely frequent the beaches and make short flights out to sea. Petrels form a large group of oceanic birds. Some petrels feed by diving into the water. But most of them fly close to the wave-tops and pick up food from the surface. Sailors call small petrels 'Mother Carey's Chickens'.

The skua is another oceanic bird. It is a fierce, robber bird, with a strong, hooked beak, and brown-and-white feathers. Far out to sea skuas will attack terns and gulls, until they surrender the food in their beaks. During the breeding season they attack anything that moves onto their territory. In the Antarctic, their diet consists of the eggs and young of penguins and other birds.

Gulls and terns are closely related birds that are found in coastal areas almost all over the world. They could be described as beach birds, although the Arctic tern makes a remarkable journey each year. It breeds in the Arctic and other northern areas, and then flies to the Antarctic for the rest of the year. Twice each year it makes a flight of about 11,000 miles.

Gulls and terns often roam far inland, especially during bad weather. Gulls are heavy birds with hooked beaks and sturdy legs. Terns are altogether more graceful, with pointed beaks, slender legs, and narrow, pointed wings and tail.

The auk family is another large group of sea birds. They are diving, fish-eating birds that live on northern sea-coasts. Auks are mainly black and white in colour and include the little auk, puffin, guillemot and razorbill.

Cormorants and shags are large, dark water birds found on seacoasts all over the world. They are distinguished from auks and divers by their hook-tipped beaks and longer tails and wings.

Divers are swimming birds that live in open waters and are almost helpless on land.

Sea-cow The sea-cow is a large, warmwater mammal that never comes on to land. Sea-cows may grow to a length of 10 to 12 feet. They have fat, ungainly bodies, with paddle-like front legs which are used for swimming. They have no back legs, but have a flat, fleshy tail. It is forked in one kind of sea-cow—the dugong—but in the other kinds—the manatees—it is round. Dugongs live in the Indian and western Pacific oceans.

Manatees live on the African and South American coasts of the Atlantic. All seacows live in shallow water and river estuaries, feeding on seaweed and other water plants. They can 'stand up' in the water, with part of their bodies above the surface. This habit, especially when they are nursing their babies, undoubtedly led to the many stories of mermaids.

Seahorse This is a small marine fish with a head that looks somewhat like a horse's head. Seahorses vary in size from four to nine inches, and have an unusual tail with which they anchor

Some common sea birds:
1. The common cormorant, the largest of the cormorants is about 36 inches long. Cormorants swim well and may stay under water for up to 30 seconds.
2. An albatross uses gusts of wind and the variable wind speed at different levels to glide above the sea surface.
3. The great skua is a swift, powerful bird. It preys on gulls, chasing them until they are forced to give up their food.
4. Puffins are members of the auk family. The puffin has a large triangular-shaped beak with which it can hold several fish at once.
5. The king shag is a member of the same family as the cormorant. It is about 20 inches long and lives in New Zealand.

Alaska fur seals at their breeding grounds on the Probilof Isles. The bull seal sits on a rock surrounded by his wives.

themselves to water plants. They are found in all the oceans of the world. There are 25 species, coloured white, yellow, red or blue.

The seahorse swims in an upright position by waving its *dorsal* (back) fin. The female lays several hundred eggs in a brood pouch on the underside of the male's body. The eggs hatch in the pouch, and the male expels the young seahorses from the pouch through a small opening.

Seals are large mammals that spend much of their life in the sea. All of them come onto the shore to breed, however. Seals are well suited to life in the water. They have streamlined bodies and pointed snouts. Instead of legs they have flippers,

The seahorse is the only fish that has a prehensile tail—it can wind its tail around seaweeds to anchor itself.

with which they can swim at great speed. Under their skin is a fatty layer of blubber, which protects them from the cold of the far northern and southern regions in which many of them live. Seals feed on fish and other sea creatures.

There are three families of seals: the true seals, the eared seals, and the walrus (see Walrus). The eared seals have small external ear-flaps, whereas the true seals simply have ear openings. The flippers of eared seals are much longer than those of true seals. As a result, the eared seals can run along on land on their flippers. True seals cannot— they have to wriggle along on their bellies. As a result they spend much less of their lives on the shore than do eared seals.

Among the true seals are the common seal of Europe and North America, which grows to about five feet in length. The male elephant seal, the biggest kind of seal, may reach a length of 20 feet and a weight of four tons—almost as much as an ordinary land elephant. The nose of an elephant seal is lengthened into a kind of 'trunk'. Other true seals include the grey seal of the Atlantic and the leopard seal of the Antarctic, which preys on penguins. The eared seals include the sea-lion, well known for its tricks in zoos and circuses.

Sea-shore A sea-shore is a rich hunting ground for the naturalist. All forms of marine life are to be found on the sea-shore, as well as the many birds that get their food there. They include the sea-gulls and other flying hunters that often nest in cliffs, and the long-legged wading birds that walk in calm shallows picking up their prey.

There are several types of sea-shore. Pebbly beaches do not contain much life. Tidal estuaries and sandy and muddy shores are a haven for animals that move about freely, feeding on other animals and plant life. Estuaries support anemones and jellyfish as well as shrimps, crabs, winkles, cockles, mussels and oysters. Common fishes found in estuaries are eels, blennies, gobies and flounders. Sandy shores yield several interesting worms on digging, including ragworms and lug-worms. Beautiful shells, such as scallops, cockles and razor shells, are common. Flat-fish may be found, and care must be taken with the weever fish, which lies in the sand with its poisonous spines protruding.

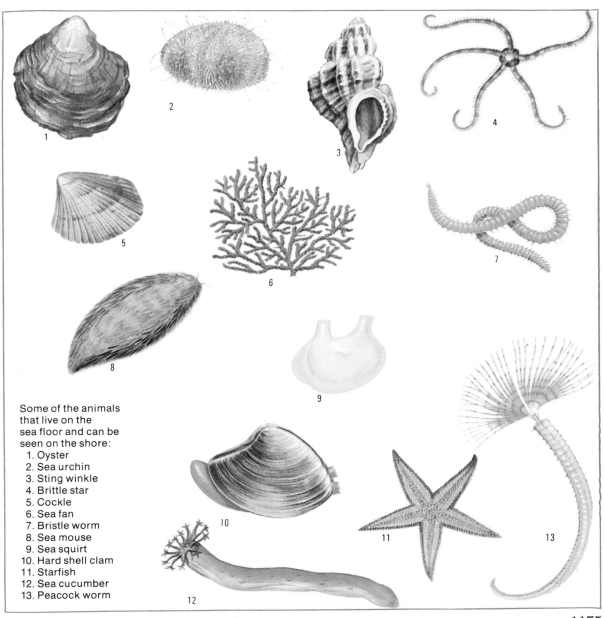

Some of the animals that live on the sea floor and can be seen on the shore:
1. Oyster
2. Sea urchin
3. Sting winkle
4. Brittle star
5. Cockle
6. Sea fan
7. Bristle worm
8. Sea mouse
9. Sea squirt
10. Hard shell clam
11. Starfish
12. Sea cucumber
13. Peacock worm

Typical Shore Animals

High Spring Tide Level
High Neap Tide Level
Mean Sea Level
Low Neap Tide Level
Low Spring Tide Level
Peacock Worms
Crabs
Anemones
Mussels
Sand Hoppers
Shore Slaters
Barnacles, Top Shells, Limpets
Splash Zone
Green Seaweed

Brown Seaweed

Red Seaweed

A diagram showing the various tide levels and zones of a rocky shore. The lighter the colour, the longer is the period of exposure to the air.

The most rewarding type of shore is a *rocky shore*. Here are found the fixed animals that cling to rocks and feed on passing animals. As the tide goes down, exposing them to the air, they close up or shut their shells, and free-moving animals withdraw into seaweed or under rocks. A few are caught in rock pools and can be easily observed. A rocky shore has several zones. At the top, above high-tide mark, is the *splash zone*. This region is splashed by spray at high tide and covered during the high spring tides. It is the home of some woodlice, sand-hoppers and winkles, with green seaweed and crabs in the pools. The *upper shore* is covered at high tide only. Bladder-wrack seaweed is found there, and lim-pets, winkles and barnacles cling to the rocks. Starfish may be found in pools.

The *middle shore*, between high and low water levels at the neap tides, is also the home of most of the animals already mentioned. On the *lower shore*, which is uncovered only at low spring tides, are found some others, such as brittle-stars, sea-urchins, squat lobsters, and prawns.

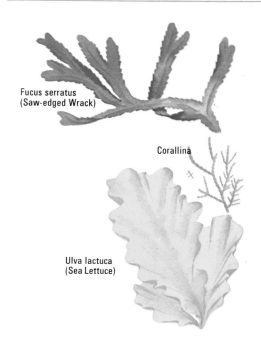

Fucus serratus (Saw-edged Wrack)

Corallina

Ulva lactuca (Sea Lettuce)

There are three main types of seaweeds — green, brown and red.

Left: Starfishes use their tube feet as suckers to pull the shells of bivalves apart to get at their flesh.

Right: Hermit crabs often shelter in the empty shells of molluscs. The anemone is often found attached to the shell in which the hermit crab lives.

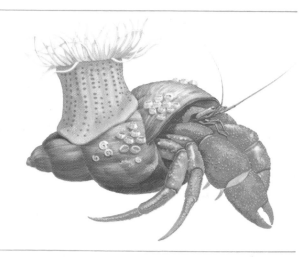

1176